Reluctantly Related

Secrets to Getting Along With Your Mother-in-Law or Daughter-in-Law

by

Deanna Brann, Ph.D.
Your In-Law Survival Guide

Illustrations by
Donald Hoenig

AMBERGRIS

Reluctantly Related:
Secrets to Getting Along with Your Mother-in-Law or Daughter-in-Law
by Deanna Brann, Ph.D.
Illustrations by Donald Hoenig

ISBN 978-0-9888100-0-6
Printed in the United States.

Library of Congress Control Number: 2013900559

AMBERGRIS
Ambergris Publishing
11124 Kingston Pike Road #119-172
Knoxville, TN 37934

In Memory
of
my sister Brenda

Acknowledgements

Part of this journey has been about accepting what I didn't know and taking that uneasy step to ask for help. I am deeply indebted to the following individuals, whose help, support, and love have made this book a reality.

I want to thank each mother-in-law, daughter-in-law, and husband/son who willingly shared his or her story with me. Although for some the sharing brought joy, to most of you it stirred up the pain and sorrow of this struggling relationship. This book could not have been written without you.

Michelle Clodfelter my daughter-in-law, whom I have loved from the time she was first in my son's life. Wanting to make our relationship better, for both of us, was what planted the "book" seed. Your support for this book helped to make it possible. I also want to thank my son Anthony Clodfelter for your love and support throughout this process. The many late-night discussions with you and Michelle were invaluable to me.

My husband Roger Monforton, who has not only been a support for me, but the one I really leaned on when I struggled, doubted and questioned this whole process. You gave me the most invaluable feedback every step of the way and willingly listened whenever I needed to talk. I love you with all my heart. Your insights, wisdom, humor, and overall ability to see things differently from me, helped to improve the quality of this book tremendously.

Don Hoenig, my cartoonist/illustrator, whose talent captured the look and spirit of my characters in every drawing. Through your skill as well as your patience you were able to take my concepts and bring them to life.

I also want to thank Katy Koontz, my editor who believed in me and my project, and my ability to get my message out. Your gift for taking my rough drafts and knowing exactly what they needed to make my message even clearer was amazing. And you "got" me, which made working with you so easy. You have an incredible gift.

My dear friend Penny Kennedy who was there when this book was just an idea in my head; your love and support has given me so many opportunities to cry, laugh, and grow from this process. Both your honesty and love have helped not only this book to be better, but has helped me to be a better person. I love you for always believing in me.

My long-time friend Sharon Hall, whose love and support was there during those dark troubling times in my relationship with Michelle. Your encouragement helped me to believe I could do something different. And most importantly, you helped to keep me grounded. I couldn't have gotten this far without you as my friend.

Contents

Part III: Patterns and Solutions

Part IV: Finishing Touches

With the exception of my story and Michelle's story, all stories and examples are not representative of any one individual or their experience, but rather they are a composite of like personalities, relationships and situations.

Part I:

The Making of the MIL-DIL Relationship

Chapter 1

The Thanksgiving From Hell

"I know you *think* you're being helpful, *but don't feed Lauren or give her a bottle,"* spat my daughter-in-law Michelle at me through her clenched teeth. Her whole body was shaking. She was furious with me.

It had all happened so innocently, but there was no convincing her of that now. I had committed the cardinal sin of feeding my newest granddaughter so that Michelle and my son, Anthony, could sleep in a little longer. Like a deer caught in a car's headlights, I was stunned. But that quickly turned to anger. They were guests in my home. I was only trying to be helpful. My defenses were up as I felt under attack.

I have to admit that I felt an undercurrent of fear, as well. Michelle might as well have said, *"Don't go near my child again!"* And the thought of her cutting my husband and me off from my son and grandchildren terrified me.

This heated exchange was the beginning of what our family has since dubbed the "Thanksgiving From Hell." On this fateful holiday morning, I had a personal wake-up call about my own mother-in-law/daughter-in-law relationship. Michelle and I had had words before, but what occurred on this day took us to a whole new level. Or rather, it sank us both to a new, all-time low.

Let me share a little background with you so you can better understand just how maddening this incident was. I had been a single mom to my only son, Anthony, for most of his growing-up years, so I'd learned to be a pretty independent and take-charge kind of woman. I met my current husband, Roger, the year Anthony and Michelle moved from Michigan (where we had all lived) to Tennessee. Roger and I tied the knot three years later – just a few years after Anthony and Michelle married.

At the time of the hellish Thanksgiving, I was also a clinical psychotherapist, although I've since retired. You might think that with more than 20 years of conducting individual, couples and family therapy, I would know how to have great relationships with ease – and I might have naively thought that once, too. Let's just say that my trouble getting along with Michelle was frustrating on more than a few levels.

It wasn't always that way. From the beginning, Michelle and I had gotten along well. I had been happy for Anthony that he had found a wonderful woman to love and spend his life with. They dated nearly five years before they got married, and during that time, my relationship with Michelle had seemed pretty solid.

That started to change when their first child, Elise, was born. Storm clouds of trouble began to gather on the horizon, and not only was I baffled by this, but I also had no clue how to get out of their path. And for reasons I did not understand, Michelle did not seem to be bothered by the brewing storm at all.

Then Lauren was born, and I had two granddaughters. By this time, Anthony and Michelle had lived in Tennessee for about seven years. And now that they had children, the fact that they lived so far away from family was even more difficult – not just for us, but for Michelle's parents (who also lived in Michigan), as well. I'm sure they missed Anthony, Michelle and the girls as much as we did.

To be fair, Anthony and Michelle had agreed when they got married to alternate whose family they spent the holidays with each year, and this particular year was Roger's and my turn to have them for Thanksgiving. They'd gotten in late the night before, and I had hoped for their sake that they would be able to sleep in for a bit.

So when I heard Lauren stir in her crib, I'd gotten her up to take her quietly downstairs so her mom and dad could sleep. And yes, when she acted hungry, feeding her and letting my son and daughter-in-law sleep in seemed like the natural and considerate thing to do. But I soon came to find out (in no uncertain terms!) that from Michelle's perspective, what I did that Thanksgiving morning was far from helpful. She saw it as intrusive, even hurtful. How is it that we could be so out of touch with each other's reality?

Michelle's Story

A few days before we left our home in Tennessee to visit our families in Michigan for the Thanksgiving holiday, I could already feel my teeth starting to clench. I love my family and am always excited to see them. But being with them also leaves me feeling a bit empty, too, as if there's a longing that is never quite satisfied – and I'm not even sure where it's coming from. Still, in the midst of being around them, I feel safe and secure for the moment.

It's not like that at all when I'm with my in-laws. My husband's mother, Deanna, is great a lot of the time. But then there are these moments – a lot of them lately, especially since the kids were born – when she really makes me doubt myself and start to feel insecure. Maybe I'm crazy, but I think sometimes she does things just to hurt me, to make it hard for me to feel good about myself or to feel like a successful mom. Anthony says she's not really doing that; she's just trying to be helpful. It's hard, though, to keep trying to give her the benefit of the doubt.

Still, we agreed years ago that we'd alternate whose family we'd spend the holidays with, and while we were going to see both of our families on this trip, we were going to spend Thanksgiving with Deanna and her husband, Roger. Oh well.

I still remember the last time Deanna came here to visit. She kept the girls while I worked all day. That was bad enough, since I'd rather have been home with them. But when I came in from work, I'd find her playing with Elise as Lauren sat next to them, cooing in her carrier. The scene was like some kind of Hallmark commercial. All the toys were neatly put away, all the dishes were done and the rest of the house was picked up, too.

I can't stand it when she does that. It's like she's showing off, proving she can handle *my* home and family better than *I* can. I try to appreciate her help, but it's hard when she just takes over everything. And then she gives me pointers on how I should do something. It's as if she's scrutinizing what I'm doing and imposing her way onto mine. I end up feeling so inadequate, so bad about myself. Then I just want to give up on the whole relationship.

As the time to start packing the car to leave for Michigan grew closer, I felt the now-familiar agitation grow inside of me. My thoughts just kept spinning. *Why doesn't Anthony just let me pack our things in the car – he doesn't do it right anyway. It looks like it's going to rain. I hate driving in the rain. Why is there always so much to do before we leave? Please don't let Lauren be getting another ear infection! What if it snows while we're there? We have no heavy coats. Do I have enough clothes for Elise? Which toys should we take? Now Anthony is driving me crazy again!*

The tension kept building as I kept dreading the nine-hour drive to Michigan. Anthony and I kept bickering, and I snapped at him far more than usual.

I knew my mom was upset that we wouldn't be spending Thanksgiving Day with her. It's not that she said anything specific, but I could tell. And having her upset always sends me into an emotional tailspin – not what I needed on top of my own tensions about the holiday weekend.

Once we were on our way, the girls settled down and the car got quiet. We drove for hours, and as we finally crossed the state line into Michigan the girls were asleep. Anthony and I tuned in to the radio station we used to listen to when we lived there. Maybe I was just homesick with all the changes in our lives and my babies growing so fast. Lauren sighed deeply in her sleep, and my mind went into overdrive. I was still nursing her, and I loved that special time we had together. But she seemed to be weaning herself far more quickly than I wanted her to. I knew that once this special time was gone, it would be gone for good, and it made my heart ache. I wanted time to slow down. I had shared some of my concerns with Anthony, but I didn't let him know the real depth of my pain – I didn't think he'd understand.

We got to Deanna and Roger's house quite late. I took a deep breath and slowly let it out. I heard Maggie, their yellow Lab, barking inside the house as I unbuckled Lauren from her car seat. Deanna and Roger helped unload the car as we took our still-sleeping girls inside. After getting the girls to bed and saying a few brief hellos, we were off to bed ourselves. It had been a long day.

I woke up around 7 the next morning, anxious to see if I could get Lauren to nurse. Even though she'd been less interested lately, I wanted to try, hoping she would. She really didn't seem to be hungry, so reluctantly I laid my daughter back down in her crib, returned to the room where Anthony and I were staying and fell back asleep.

Around 8:30, I woke up again and thought I'd give it another try with Lauren. I went into the room where her crib was, but she wasn't there. The anger began to surge through me. I knew it! Deanna must have taken her downstairs. She must be feeding her. *She did it again!* I thought angrily. *We've just barely arrived at her house, and she's already trying to take over. She makes me feel so inadequate. Why does she have to be that way? Why couldn't she have asked before she just took Lauren?* I immediately went into our room. Needing to vent and feel validated, I woke Anthony. Without giving him a chance to say anything, I started to spew out my anger.

"She took Lauren downstairs," I told him. "I *know* she must be feeding her. *You* need to say something to your mom. *You* need to tell her she should ask first."

Anthony was only half awake and wasn't sure what had happened or what had triggered my rage, but what he did know was that my anger was escalating. He wanted to try to defuse the growing rage, but he knew from past experience that any attempts he'd make would probably be futile. And he was still tired from working and then making the long drive the day before.

"It's just one feeding," he said, trying to calm me down. "Don't make a big deal out of it. Just try to forget about it for now."

His words felt like a sudden slap in the face. My husband was not going to rescue me. He was not going to step up to the plate and deal with his mother. Now I was not only furious at Deanna, but I was also just as angry with Anthony. My heart was racing more than ever as my rage took over every ounce of my being. *I need to handle this myself,* I thought, seething with resentment. *I can't let her get away with this.*

I marched downstairs determined to speak up for myself. Deanna was in the kitchen. I knew she had seen me come in, but she acted as though she hadn't. Finally, she looked up. I couldn't contain myself. I needed her to know that what she had done was not OK and that she had overstepped her bounds – again. I knew my words were accusatory, but I didn't care because that was how I felt.

"Did you feed her?" I demanded to know. I could see it in Deanna's face – she was stunned. *Good,* I thought, knowing I had made my point. I'm not sure she had a chance to speak, but even if she started, I am sure I cut her off because I needed to finish this. I needed to let her know how I felt.

"I know you *think* you're being helpful," I said, my anger obvious. "But don't feed Lauren or give her a bottle." I started to go on, but I saw Deanna's face change. I had seen this look before. I knew I had stepped over the line, but I couldn't go back. I didn't know *how* to go back. It was too late. We both started saying things to each other, although I can't for the life of me remember what either one of us said. But there was no stopping.

Suddenly, I saw Anthony in the hallway. *Good,* I thought to myself. *He'll tell her that she needs to stop, that she needs to back off.* But he didn't. He told us both to stop, and then he walked away. My husband walked away! I was crushed. How could he do that to me? How could he just walk away, saying nothing to his mother? To me, that was the same as siding with her and not standing up for *me.* I felt so betrayed. Now, Deanna was angry with me, my husband had abandoned me and I just felt so alone. All I wanted to do at that point was go to my mom's house.

Deanna ran upstairs to her bedroom, leaving me standing there. But I felt I needed to vindicate myself. I at least wanted Anthony to know that I wasn't the one who started this. I wasn't the one at fault here. So I quickly climbed the stairs to the guest bedroom and sat on the bed. Looking at my husband, I pleaded my case.

"All I wanted was for her to *ask,*" I tried to explain. "That's all I tried to tell her, and she just went off on me ... ." I hadn't even had a chance to get dressed yet, and already I had spent *more* than enough time with my mother-in-law for one visit.

My Story

I still shudder when I remember that day. I have to be honest – although I love the kids and was looking forward to seeing them, I'd also been dreading their visit quite a bit, for the same reasons that Michelle had been. I couldn't figure out what it was that I always seemed to do that would make her so angry, but I felt like whatever I did was always wrong in her eyes. And we couldn't ever talk about it.

I think the tension started right after their oldest, Elise, was born. I had flown down for 10 days to help out. Elise hadn't started daycare yet, but both Anthony and Michelle had to be back at work. I took care of the baby all day, cleaned the house and cooked meals. I expected that since I'd done all that, Michelle would at least pitch in to clean up after dinner. But she was tired after her long day at work, and she wanted to let the dishes go until later. Letting dirty dishes sit around was a foreign concept to me.

I guess I didn't feel appreciated, and it stung. So I'd gotten snippy. Michelle pointed out that she hadn't *asked* me to do all those things in the first place. Then she let loose a barrage of stored-up criticism, accusing me of being intrusive, pushy and controlling. This was really hard to take because my intentions had been the exact opposite of all her accusations – I had been trying to make things *easier* on her, not more difficult. Tension hung in the air for the rest of my visit, and it became the first of many such altercations.

After a blow-up with Michelle, I could never understand how she could view me the way she did. Didn't she understand that I just wanted to be helpful and that I just wanted to give her something *I* never got from my family? I'd end up feeling a bit stunned – as well as confused, annoyed and frustrated, to say the least. I constantly felt as if I were walking on eggshells around her – not having any idea what would set her off next.

That was part of what was so maddening – I couldn't predict when these incidents were going to happen. Sometimes, Michelle and I were able to connect as we'd done before, and we'd even have some great talks together. We'd have so much fun, and then I would feel such hope! So I'd let my guard down. But then, without warning, we'd suddenly have another blow-up over something stupid. She'd act as though she hated me again, and we'd end up screaming at each other. We seemed to keep diving back into a black hole that we couldn't find our way out of. It was a *nightmare*.

We couldn't ever talk about our relationship problems. Sometimes I'd try, but it was always awkward and tense, and that made my words sound even more forceful. Then we would inevitably get sucked back down into *that hole* again. So against my better judgment, I usually just ended up letting the whole issue slide, hoping that the next time, things between us would be different. Here I was, a clinical psychotherapist who prided myself on my communication skills and my ability to help people work through family issues, but I couldn't talk to my own daughter-in-law about our problems or do anything to make them better. The whole situation left me feeling utterly powerless, not to mention absolutely *crazy*!

Making it even more excruciating was the fact that I was always afraid that Michelle might really go off the deep end and sever all ties with me – even though she didn't really give me any concrete reason to believe this. The thought of losing my relationship with my son (my only child) and my granddaughters forever was simply more than I could bear. That fear *haunted* me. I felt I had so much at stake that each time a get-together approached, my stomach would churn, my anxiety would build, my heart would race and I would anticipate the *worst*. I would be emotionally exhausted before I even said hello.

That fateful Thanksgiving visit was certainly no exception. The week before Anthony, Michelle and the girls arrived, I couldn't sleep for worrying about what it would be like this time. I found myself anxiously anticipating, and I just felt raw emotionally.

I had good reason to worry because I knew they really didn't like coming to visit – Anthony disliked it even more than Michelle, and our frequent blow-ups didn't help. It was easy for me to blame their reluctance to visit on how hard it can be to travel with a kindergartner and an infant, but I knew that wasn't really it.

The real reasons that they didn't like visiting us started long before they ever left home. First, Michelle felt guilty for living so far away from her family, and this feeling seemed to grow whenever she was in town. She seemed constantly impatient to be with them when she was here, and it began to fuel a real sense of competition between her mother and me for their time and attention. Add to that the stress both Anthony and Michelle felt in trying to please everyone – yet knowing they couldn't possibly succeed.

We all understood the alternating holiday rules, but the stress of knowing we would have to keep to a strict schedule (Thanksgiving with us, but exactly half of their time with Michelle's family, too) added to the tension that was already brewing.

They arrived late of course, with the long drive, and after we greeted them and exchanged a few pleasantries, we all turned in for the night. The girls slept in a room just across the hall from their parents. Elise was 5 years old, and Lauren was just 7 months. In our brief discussion before going to bed, none of us brought up what would transpire in the morning – what time people wanted to get up, what the morning routine would be, and so on.

Those questions were in the back of my mind, but thinking about them made my head start to spin and my anxiety rise. If I asked about what was going to happen in the morning, I figured, I was sure to be seen as intrusive or as trying to take something away from Michelle. But if I said nothing, I risked doing something that would make her angry. And so I waited for Michelle, or even Anthony, to say something about the morning. Neither said a word.

The next day, Roger and I were up by 6:30, although everyone else was still asleep. We sat at the kitchen table together drinking coffee. Around 7:30, we heard Lauren start to stir in her crib, so we talked about what we should do. Should we get her up, or should we wait for Anthony or Michelle to do that? Although I was all for spending time with Lauren, I was hesitant. I knew that our decision, whatever it would be, could very easily cause a problem, and that problem could blow up in my face.

In fact, I seemed to have caused lots of "problems" over the previous five years. I'd always end up wondering whether I should do what made sense to me, or whether I should just do nothing so as not to offend. No matter what approach I ended up taking, neither really seemed to work well for me or for Michelle. We'd typically find ourselves back in the black hole. It was painful – for *both* of us. And always in the back of my mind, I would worry that Michelle would end up keeping my grand-daughters *and* my son away from me. The very thought horrified me.

So when Lauren awoke, I debated what to do. I really liked the idea of Roger and me having some time with Lauren by ourselves. Our visits to Tennessee were usually over holidays, so whatever we did with the girls typically included at least one of their parents, if not both. We might get a few minutes alone with the girls if we went on a walk with them or took them to a park, but the chance to have some time simply to hang out seemed wonderful. Plus, we knew Anthony and Michelle never had a chance to sleep in or get a break from parenting because no family members on either side lived remotely close to them at that time.

The choice seemed clear. We'd get Lauren up, change her, give her some breakfast if she wanted it and just hang out with her. Michelle had put bottles of formula and breast milk in the refrigerator the night before. I also had some jars of baby food and some cereal available. So I went upstairs, got Lauren out of bed, changed her and brought her down to the family room, where we spent time holding her until she was a bit more awake.

After a while, Lauren became fussy. She seemed hungry, so I grabbed a bottle of the refrigerated breast milk without being sure if I should give her that or the formula. She must have been hungry because she drank the whole bottle. She acted as though she still wanted something, so Roger gave her small pieces of banana and a little cereal. As she did with the milk, Lauren ate everything we put in front of her. Once she finished her breakfast, we spent some time playing with her. She smiled and cooed. It was great. All three of us were having a wonderful time – Roger and I were getting to know Lauren, and Lauren was getting to know us. Between 8:30 and 9, Lauren started getting a little sleepy, so I took her upstairs and laid her back down.

Roger has an unusual Thanksgiving Day tradition he's followed forever – he and several of his friends get together in the morning to play a little ice hockey, a very big sport in Michigan. So after I put Lauren back down, Roger packed up his hockey gear and left for the rink. It was quiet in the house. I thought everyone else was still sleeping, so I decided to take that time to start preparing a few things for our Thanksgiving dinner.

As I cut up the apples for apple pie, I was thinking both about my morning with Lauren as well as the day ahead, although I was focusing on food preparation more than on anything else. Then I caught a glimpse of someone coming around the corner from the hallway into the kitchen. Engrossed in the apples, I didn't look up, but out of the corner of my eye, I could tell it was Michelle. I could sense from her body language that she was very upset about something. It was quite obvious. My heart started to race. Anxiety began to surge through my body.

My first reaction was to keep my focus on what I was doing, pretending I didn't notice her mood. *Maybe it's just my imagination. Maybe everything is fine*, I nervously tried to convince myself. Yet my anxiety clearly won out as questions started scrambling in my head: *What did I do? Was it something I said last night? Was I being too loud in the kitchen this morning?* I could think of nothing I had done that would cause Michelle to be upset.

Before I could tell Michelle about the morning – our desire to let them sleep in, changing Lauren, giving her a bottle and some breakfast – Michelle looked at me with a tense expression and a firmly set jaw.

"I know you *think* you're being helpful, *but don't feed Lauren or give her a bottle*," she spat out with a tone I knew only too well. I don't remember her words sounding necessarily loud or mean, yet their intensity pierced me in such a way that they took my breath away. It didn't matter. Michelle continued, her voice escalating, gaining momentum. Suddenly, I felt as though I was a child being scolded by her mother. I was so rattled that I could barely hear her words.

"I need to keep track of what she had – breast milk or formula. And I need to keep track of how much she is eating. So in the future, just let me take care of her," she shot back at me.

Oh my God, I thought, *I can't believe this is happening!* It was too much for me. My emotions already had been churning from anticipating the tension the day before. And now this, at the very start of the visit! I was deeply hurt, but all I could allow myself to feel at the time was the protectiveness of anger. And I *really* felt angry. My need to respond immediately – to defend myself and justify my actions – was overwhelming. I reacted, the words flying out of my mouth before I could stop them in a voice that was loud, strong and more intense than I ever knew was possible.

"Look, I'm a mother, too," I yelled. "I *know* you think I don't remember what to do. But I *do*. I just wanted to let you sleep in, get some rest and have some time off ... ."

And then I saw it in her face. I had done it. I had pushed us over the edge into that black hole we so often tumbled into. At that point, Michelle couldn't hear what I was saying. Just as I had reacted to her strong tone, she was now reacting to mine.

"She's my child, and this is what I want!" she lashed out.

And so we continued helplessly spiraling further into *that hole*, headfirst and at high speed. It felt as though we had been caught spiraling in that vortex for a lifetime. And I was certain that we were never, ever going to be able to get out of it.

Suddenly, I saw my son standing in the hallway. Michelle and I had been going back and forth so intensely that I hadn't even heard Anthony come down the stairs. He looked tired, but I could tell from his expression that he was not just annoyed, he was *angry*.

"What are you two fighting about?" he demanded.

Although I don't think Anthony really wanted an answer, both Michelle and I started talking at the same time, defending our positions, looking to him to tell us who was right and who was wrong. He did neither. He shook his head in disgust, turned to go back upstairs and mumbled as he walked away, "This is why I hate coming to Michigan."

I felt defeated. I was hurt, embarrassed and angry – yet all I could do was cry. There was nothing more to say. Michelle and I were at a standoff, and I knew I had already lost more than I could ever gain if I continued. I couldn't stay there any longer. Without another word I left Michelle standing in the hallway. I ran upstairs to my bedroom, closed the door and sat on my bed, staring at the floor. After a long moment, I looked up at the clock, shook my head in hopeless disbelief and sobbed. It was barely 10 a.m.

Chapter 2

Why the MIL-DIL Relationship Is So Hard

Mother-in-law/daughter-in-law relationships can certainly be challenging, even if they aren't always as painful, stressful and confusing as my relationship was on that particular Thanksgiving. Some in-law relationships can be really good, some can be just OK (but you wish they were better), some (you realize with resignation) are pretty much as good as it gets, and then you have those that are downright horrible.

If you are one of the lucky ones, and your relationship has been good from the start, then *bravo* to you and your mother-in-law or daughter-in-law. However, if you fall into any of the other categories – from being just OK all the way to having nuclear meltdown potential – know that with some expert advice, direction and the right tools, you can totally transform your relationship.

But before you start transforming anything, let's take a look at why this in-law relationship is both so difficult and so different from all your other relationships. Becoming aware of the *why* helps put some of these highly charged experiences into perspective so they don't seem quite so ominous and foreboding. And that helps you start to shift how you feel about your relationship with your in-law. So now let's examine the five reasons the mother-in-law/daughter-in-law relationship is so difficult.

The Artificial Element

Even the closest mother-in-law/daughter-in-law relationships start out artificially. I mean, the two of you aren't really *family* (as we usually think of related family members), and you aren't yet *friends*, but you are certainly more than casual acquaintances! So what the heck *is* this relationship anyway?

To answer that question, let's first take a look at friendships. When you make a friend, it's usually because something between the two of you clicks. You have common interests, common beliefs and common values. Or maybe you have similar backgrounds or family histories. Whatever makes the two of you click, you probably feel pretty much like equals. At the very least, each of you feels she is getting something beneficial from the other and that over time there's a genuine give-and-take between you. The key here is the phrase *over time*. Rarely do friendships develop immediately. I won't say that *never* happens, but the truth is that it doesn't happen all that often.

But when you look at the mother-in-law/daughter-in-law relationship (which I'll refer to as the MIL-DIL relationship from now on), what you see is something else altogether. When your son marries, or when you marry, you immediately have a new "family." When the bride says, "I take this man ..." what is really happening is that she's taking this man *and his family*, including his mother, for better or for worse. So in this case, one plus one does not equal two, but usually at least six.

Even if you've known your in-laws for years, you are not officially family prior to saying "I do." When things become legal, the new MIL and DIL are thrown together because of only one thing – her son or her husband. Whether you think your new in-law is marvelous, mediocre or mean, the fact remains that you didn't get to choose her.

If you're the DIL, then you chose your husband, with his family being part of the package (just as your family is part of the package for him). And if you're like most people, you probably didn't put much thought into what your relationship with your new family would be like. Your focus has been on your new life with your new husband. Fair enough!

If you're the MIL, you raised your son in the best way you knew how, teaching him from childhood about making good choices. Yet you didn't get to vote on his choice of a wife. Your son chose her all by himself. And this means that the relationship you have with your in-law really begins as an artificial relationship, with the only guaranteed thing you have in common being your son or husband.

The two of you begin forging a relationship before you really have a chance – or even a desire – to know who the other one is as an individual. It's a bit like going on a blind date, except the other person automatically ends up reappearing in your life on a regular basis, whether or not you hit it off. And all this relationship forging needs to happen *fast* – even if you've been around each other for a fair amount of time before the marriage. After all, everything is different now. Being a wife and DIL is *not* the same thing as being a girlfriend. And this difference is every bit as real for the MIL.

Different Stages, Different Emotional Places

The second factor that can make MIL-DIL rapport a struggle is that you and your in-law are at different stages in your lives. Because of your MIL status, you've already done the things your DIL is just beginning to do. You've been a grown woman for some time now; you have already chosen your path as a wife and mother, and you've chosen a career, whether you stayed home or worked outside the home. You may be married or you may be divorced. Regardless, you've already made a home and a life of your own. At this point, you are likely to feel as

though you are in a position to create a
new identity around what it means to be
a woman, a wife, a mother, a grandmother,
etc. And you may also be creating an
identity around new interests, hobbies,
career and friendships.

As a DIL, on the other hand, you're
just beginning your new life as a wife, a
grown woman and possibly a future mother.
You're still figuring out how to fit all these
things into your life along with figuring
out who *you* are as an adult with your
own interests, goals and career path. No matter how put-together you
may be, you're still in the early stages of coming into your own.
Establishing yourself as an adult is important to you. You're looking
forward to creating a home of your very own and a life with your
husband. You need the time to do it your way, and suddenly having another
mother figure in your life can potentially complicate the entire adventure.

To add another layer, both of you are in different emotional places.
The MIL sees life very differently now than when she was her DIL's age.
Because of the journey she's already taken and the relationships she's
developed or maintained over the years, she could have ended up being
a little sad, a little bitter, maybe wiser or even more easy-going. And in
all likelihood, the MIL is probably pretty set in her ways as a mature
woman. On the other hand, she could be unsure of where she is now that
her roles are needing to change.

As for the DIL, she is just beginning to create her life. She is
looking forward. She's carving out her place in the world, focusing on
her dreams and strengthening her partnership with her husband. She wants
to do things and is figuring out how she wants to do them. She is filled
with optimism, hope and excitement about her new life and her journey
into the future. Perhaps she's a bit anxious about all the choices ahead of
her and about doing things "right," but she's excited nonetheless about
what life has in store.

Being at different life stages and in different emotional places can
make it hard for the two of you to have a lot in common with each other.

You end up both trying to figure out – often independently – how to make "this thing" between you work as best you can. It's often a bit like entering a three-legged race with someone who is much taller or much shorter than you are. It's almost impossible to move forward smoothly and easily because one person naturally has a much longer stride than the other. With the MIL-DIL relationship, it often seems too much like one is the teacher and the other is the student; or worse, one is the parent and the other is the child. Ugh! This definitely doesn't feel good, especially to a DIL.

Personal History and Carry-On Baggage

A third factor playing into why the MIL-DIL relationship is so difficult is that you both come into this relationship with your own history and your own emotional baggage (as you do in any relationship). In other words, you have different personal issues because you've been through different challenges or situations in your lives.

For example, let's look at what might happen if you grew up with a mother who was depressed. If this were the case, your mother probably wouldn't have made much of an effort to really connect with you emotionally while you were growing up. She might have taken care of all your physical needs, but she probably wasn't able to give you much emotional support. As a child, then, you probably would have felt as though you were invisible or as if you'd done something wrong to make your mother not like you very much. So you might have spent a lot of time wanting your mother to "see" you, to feel as though you mattered. Intellectually, you may have known she loved you and that you were important to her, but it wouldn't have felt that way on the inside.

That wouldn't have been the end of the story, though. This yearning or longing to be seen or to matter wouldn't just magically go away because you become an adult. This feeling would follow you into your adult relationships, where the same feelings would often replay themselves.

Inevitably, everyone's childhood "stuff" will come up. (In this example, you might end up in relationships with men who are also emotionally unavailable, even if their reasons for being unavailable are different from the reasons your mother had.) And when this stuff does come up, you will tend to *feel* the same way you did as a child. So you'll probably *respond* the same way you did when you were a child, too. More emotional twists ensue depending on whether the other person is younger or older than you are, and whether the unavailable parent was male or female. Wow! The un-fun possibilities are endless.

Perception Is Reality, Right?

Now we've come to the fourth factor in the MIL-DIL relationship: perception.

Perception is a funny thing. Our perceptions may or may not have anything to do with reality, but they sure *feel* real to us. The wild card is that we often have *no idea* just how much our emotional baggage affects how we see ourselves as well as how we react to others. We honestly believe that the way we look at things is the way it really is – it's The Truth. But in reality, each of us is looking at the world through tinted lenses – and while yours might be rose colored, your in-law's may be amber. It can make a *huge* difference.

So imagine, for example, that thanks to your own personal history, the baggage you carry around leaves you often doubting yourself, constantly questioning yourself and generally not feeling comfortable with yourself. It's easy to see how that particular mix of issues would affect how you react to others. And this would make having relationships with certain people – including your in-law – challenging and even downright stressful. Now imagine that you grew up feeling comfortable with who you are, liking yourself (for the most part) and trusting your thoughts, feelings and judgments. In this scenario, the past wouldn't have as big an effect on the way you react to others. This is true for both MILs and DILs.

Now let me show you what this looks like with an in-law relationship. First, let's look at this example of a DIL talking with her MIL:

Here, the DIL has found a great new babysitter and is excited to tell her MIL about her find. She has no hidden agenda with her MIL. She and her husband have always wanted to have other options for babysitting because they didn't want to burden either set of grandparents or make anyone feel obligated. She and her husband see this as being responsible adults and parents.

On the other hand, the MIL feels that when her DIL hired a babysitter, the DIL took something away from her. The MIL feels that, for whatever reason, her son and his wife don't want *her* to watch the kids. The MIL is unsure of her new role since her son married. Although she and her friends talk about it, she still can't figure out where she fits. The DIL doesn't seem to need her in the way she had thought (or maybe hoped) that she would, and this definitely makes the MIL feel a bit uncertain.

Now let's look at another example of a potential MIL-DIL exchange:

This scenario shows a DIL talking with her MIL. To the MIL, they are just two women chatting. She's not really thinking about what she's saying or, more importantly, how she's saying it. She's talking as she would with one of her friends. However, her DIL sees her as having a very strong personality, and she can't hear what her MIL is saying because all she hears is her MIL criticizing or correcting her – like her own mother used to (and maybe even still does). She can't really put her finger on why she's experiencing her MIL this way; she just feels it. And although the DIL isn't consciously connecting the dots, the bottom line is that whatever her MIL is saying (or how she's saying it) is stirring up old feelings inside the DIL.

As you can see, not only do different people have different perceptions of the same encounter, but also, because of those different perceptions, things can get a bit messy. Our intentions aren't necessarily obvious to the other person. What we think we are communicating is not always what the other person hears. Again, we filter everything we hear and see through our past experiences – positive or negative. And these experiences shape who we are and how we perceive new experiences – as well as how we react.

So in both of the scenarios above, the woman speaking has nothing but the best of intentions toward the other. But the other woman has a strong and rather unpleasant reaction because of her own specific history and baggage.

There's Reacting, and Then There's *Reacting!*

You probably can guess by now that the fifth facet to relationships is the way we *react* to what we perceive. Just as our perception can be skewed, our reaction can also sometimes be a bit off. We all want to believe that our perceptions and reactions are the *only* way to see a situation and the *only* way to react to it, but unfortunately that is rarely, if ever, the case.

Let's say someone gives you a compliment, saying, "Wow, you did a really great job with that project," or "You look terrific today … love your haircut!" You will typically react in one of three ways. You might accept the compliment, believing it to be true because you know yourself well. Or you'll dismiss it as totally untrue because you don't believe that about yourself (thanks to your own personal baggage). Or, if you are transitioning between these two extremes, you may think about the compliment for a bit and begin to feel that what the other person said may have some merit.

What about when you hear something that could be construed as a criticism? If someone accuses you of being a control freak or asks, "Why did you do *that*?," your tendency will be, again, to react in one of several ways. You might take what the other person said as a criticism – proof that you're a bad person or that you've done something bad or wrong because you don't feel good about yourself. Or you might dismiss the comment either as inaccurate (because it doesn't fit with what you know about yourself) or inconsequential (because it's just someone else's perception), with no negative connotation attached. Or again, if you're transitioning between these two extremes, you may think about the comment or question and look inside yourself to see if there is any truth in it.

Let me show some examples of how reaction comes into play with in-law relationships. In the first example, the DIL is frustrated and the MIL is angry:

In the next example, the MIL stands her ground and the DIL is exasperated:

In both instances, the MILs and the DILs are reacting to each other. When one of them did or said something, the other one perceived those actions based on her own history and baggage and then reacted accordingly. But it doesn't stop there – it keeps going. In fact, it often snowballs. If the MIL says something that the DIL perceives as an attack, and the DIL reacts accordingly, then the MIL reacts to her DIL's reaction. It can continue back and forth like this (sometimes within the same conversation, and sometimes in several conversations over time) until both the MIL and the DIL are so upset with each other that neither can see straight. It becomes such a negative spiral that it becomes impossible for either woman to find her way out.

Now you may be thinking, *My situation isn't that bad. We don't have those kinds of negative spiral things.* And I believe you. However, that doesn't mean you don't perceive something differently than your in-law intended and then react in a way that reflects this misperception. Think of how you perceive and react to your in-law as though these things are on a continuum – one end is where you perceive her actions accurately and react accordingly, and the other end is where your perceptions and reactions are completely off the mark. You and your MIL or DIL may belong at either end of this continuum or somewhere in the middle. But the place where you usually find yourself on that continuum is going to determine what kind of MIL-DIL relationship you have. It's not the *only* factor in determining your relationship, but it does play a *huge* role.

ON TARGET

COMPLETELY OFF THE MARK

So let's take a moment to list these five powerful factors influencing the relationship between you and your in-law:
1) finding your way in what is initially an artificial relationship
2) being in different stages along life's journey *and* being in entirely different emotional places
3) bringing your personal history and baggage along with you
4) having your own perception of various situations
5) reacting to your in-law's behavior based on those perceptions

Yikes! How could you *not* expect things to be at least a little bumpy at times? But hold on – there's hope. The more you understand what is going on under the surface of the MIL-DIL dynamic, the greater your chances are of sidestepping the land mines along the way and ultimately enjoying the journey.

Part II:

The Characters

Introduction to the Characters

Now that you have a better understanding about *why* this relationship is so difficult, let's take a closer look at the people involved in the MIL-DIL relationship and how their personality and unique characteristics make interacting with them ... well, interesting, to say the least.

But before we begin, I want to emphasize that not two but *four* people are always involved in the dynamics of any MIL-DIL relationship.

In addition to the MIL and DIL, the husband/son and the DIL's mother also play a major role (even if the DIL's mother is no longer living or doesn't have a lot of contact with her daughter for whatever reason). Although she affects this relationship indirectly, the DIL's mother still has a huge impact on how well her daughter's MIL-DIL relationship gels.

This is true because, as you read in Chapter 2, we are *all* influenced by our own personal histories – the people in our lives as well as the events we've experienced. So a DIL's relationship with her own mother affects how she feels about herself, which in turn affects how she perceives (and reacts to) other women. On the flip side, the MIL's ability to let go of her son, allowing him to separate from her, not only allows her to move into a new and different role with him, but it also allows him to move into adulthood as a male.

The chapters in this section of the book describe the different characters found in the different MIL-DIL relationships. Chapter 3 presents the four different MIL characters, including Comfortable Carla, Mothering Margaret, Off-the-Wall Wanda and Uncertain Sara. Then, Chapter 4 introduces the four DIL characters: Confident Connie, Doubting Donna, Weird Wendy and Transitioned Tracy. Finally, Chapter 5 delves into the three different kinds of husbands/sons, including Self-Assured Andy, In-the-Middle Michael and Struggling Steven.

While reading the descriptions of these different characters, you will get a sense of who you are, who your in-law is and who your husband/ son is in this relationship. When you're reading about your own role, whether you're a MIL or a DIL, please try to think in terms of how your *in-law* perceives you, *not* how you perceive yourself. In other words, you may *think* you're in one particular in-law category, but would your MIL or DIL see you as that particular character as well? Or would she perceive you as a different one?

You may find that you, your in-law, or your husband or son fit into more than one of these descriptions. Don't be baffled by this. It is bound to happen. We tend to react to people depending on how they interact with us and what is going on with us at the time – and this can change. However, you probably will find that each of you fits into one of these character types more clearly or more often than you do the others.

If you get stuck or you're on the fence between two choices, just flip to the appendix at the end of the book. There you'll find a questionnaire and scoring key (there's one for MILs and one for DILs) that will help you nail the right identity.

Chapter 3

Mothers-in-Law

This chapter describes the four basic types of mother-in-law personalities, complete with stories and examples for each so you can see how
they act and even hear how they speak. As you read these descriptions,
you'll likely find elements of more than one type that fit, but if you're
like most people, one will hit home more than the others. We'll start out
with the preferred type, Comfortable Carla, and then we'll move on to
the more problematic types – Mothering Margaret, Off-the-Wall Wanda
and Uncertain Sara.

Comfortable Carla

Comfortable Carla is the MIL we all hope to
have or hope to be – or both! She's got it all together
because her sense of herself has broadened beyond
her role as a mother. Also, she's very aware that she
plays a *new* role in her son's life. In other words, Carla's identity is no
longer wrapped tightly around being a mom. She was there for her son as
he was growing up, guiding him, teaching him and standing beside him
as he learned to make choices (both good and bad). Although Carla did
not always agree or like the choices or decisions her son made, she

let him make them, mistakes and all, hoping or knowing he'd learn from them.

Letting go of her mother role was a gradual process – one that took years. On some level, whether consciously or unconsciously, Comfortable Carla recognized that her job as a parent was to help her son become a self-sufficient, independent-thinking man. So as her son moved through life's different stages and matured, she began shifting her focus to other roles and other interests. These other activities and hobbies now help Carla become more than just a mother. They help her gain a clearer sense of who *she* is, and they help her become comfortable with that person. For example:

> Carla had always worked outside the home. However, it wasn't until her son moved into a college dorm that she decided she finally had time to pursue something she'd always wanted to do – photography. So she enrolled in a photography class through the continuing-education department at the community college. Carla had thought about doing this for years, but she could never seem to make it happen before. Now seems like the perfect time!

Expanding her identity beyond her "mother" role helps Comfortable Carla move away from the need to see herself only as her son's mother. Yet this is just one aspect of Carla's transformation. Carla also recognizes that along with this shift in her role, the influence and importance she once had in her son's life is shifting as well – and she accepts this with grace and even pride for a mothering job well done.

No longer is Carla her son's primary source of influence or importance. No longer does he turn to her for guidance or approval. He is making his own way in life through his own decisions. When he got married, he shifted his focus even more – to his wife. Carla became aware that she no longer has the same privileges she may have had as a mother. Appropriately, her role in his life is now secondary.

Mothering Margaret

Mothering Margaret, unlike Comfortable Carla, has no intention of stepping aside – gracefully or otherwise. She continues to see herself as a primary figure in her son's life. She hangs on to the mother role either because she doesn't realize her role needs to change or because she is simply afraid of letting go and not being so important. She believes that the emotional connection she and her son had while he was growing up should be as strong now as it was when he was a child. And in some ways she continues to see him as a child. It's not that she babies him or even that her son is a mama's boy. It's more that she believes she knows him better than anyone; she believes she understands him better than anyone; and she believes she can be helpful. For example:

> While Margaret is talking with her son on the phone, she notices that he sounds tired. She mentions this to him, and he says that he thinks he's coming down with a cold or flu. Before he can say another word, Margaret suggests several things he should do to remedy his symptoms. He comments that it's just a cold and that he's fine. But Margaret continues doling out advice, believing that if she keeps going, he'll eventually agree to one of her suggestions. At one point she even says she'll bring him some cold medicine on her way home.

Mothering Margaret feels an inner turmoil, and she struggles with it. Although this turmoil is the result of her unresolved feelings about her changing role and her changing relationship with her son, she is not necessarily making that connection. This causes her to feel as though she's in a push-pull relationship with her DIL. On the other hand, Margaret may hold on tighter to her mom role – and not just with her son. After all, if she feels she needs to continue to be in the mother role with her son, she may also feel she needs to do the same with her DIL. Here's an example:

Margaret is at the store and sees a few good deals that her son and DIL could use; she goes ahead and buys the items, thinking, *They'll be so happy with what I found. I can't wait to show them.* On her way home, she decides to stop by their house and drop off her purchases. She pulls up to their house and realizes neither one of them is home. Not wanting to come back later, Margaret opens the door with the key they gave her and puts the things on the counter. While she's there, she sees a note her DIL wrote about their daughter having a sleepover and their son having a soccer game on the same day at the same time. Without thinking, Margaret jots down a note alongside her DIL's that reads, "I would be happy to take one of them to their activity if it would help."

In this situation, Mothering Margaret sees nothing wrong with her actions because she thinks she's just being a good mom. But there's something more going on as well. Lurking beneath Margaret's sense of being helpful and a good mother is an intense fear that she might possibly lose her son altogether. And while this feeling may waver between being below the surface and being right on the surface, Margaret *is* aware of its presence, and it most definitely affects her actions when she's around her DIL and even her son.

You see, Mothering Margaret feels that she and her son are no longer as close as they once were. And in her mind, the only difference is that now her son is married. So she believes her son's wife is the one who is causing this change. As a result, she feels angry that her DIL is taking her son away from her, not letting them spend time together as they once did. She's not only hanging on to her role as mother with her son, but she's also feeling competitive with her DIL. Yikes, what an unwitting mess! Here's an example:

Margaret is going over to her son and DIL's house for dinner. Although no one said anything about bringing food, Margaret decides to make her son's favorite dish and bring it with her. She knows her DIL rarely makes it for him, so she thinks it will be a nice surprise. When she gets there, she sees that dinner is almost ready. She sets her dish on the stove and lets her DIL know that she brought something over to add to the meal. Her DIL looks at it, responds with an inaudible reply and continues with what she is doing. The tension in the room is now heavy, and yet no one says a word.

Off-the-Wall Wanda

Off-the-Wall Wanda comes across as mean, insensitive and self-centered. True to her name, she can display extreme behavior. Everything seems to be about her – what she wants, how she feels or how someone has hurt, ignored or upset her in some way. She says things without thinking how her words might affect another person. Overall, her behavior makes it difficult for anyone to have a genuine relationship with her.

Someone like Off-the-Wall Wanda is not a self-reflective kind of person. Whenever she has an emotion, she just automatically reacts. And because she is not self-reflective, her feelings are extremely uncomfortable to her and she will do anything to get them to go away. So her actions are all about making herself feel better, or just making the bad feelings disappear. She doesn't concern herself with how anyone else feels because how she feels at that moment is all that matters to her.

Because of this, Wanda appears as though she's trying to control everyone and everything around her, as though she's thoughtless or just downright mean. Often she displays the extreme or off-the-wall behavior in a loud, obnoxious manner. For example:

Saying Wanda is upset that her son and DIL won't be staying all day for the upcoming big family reunion is an understatement. She heard their reasoning, but she's not buying it. The only thing running through her mind is, *How can they do this to me?* She calls her son and DIL on the phone, not really caring which one answers. She just needs to let them know they *have* to stay for the whole event. When one of them answers the phone, without even waiting to hear a "hello," Wanda shrieks into the receiver, *"How could you do this to me? What were you thinking? I can't believe you're not staying for the whole reunion!"*

Her DIL is the one who happens to pick up the phone. As she listens to Wanda's attacking questions, she closes her eyes, takes a deep breath and composes herself. As calmly as she can, she says, "Wanda, we're just walking out the door, we'll have to call you … ."

But without waiting for her DIL to finish, Wanda snaps, "You *have* to stay for the reunion. Some of the family won't be getting there until after you leave. I told them you would be there. *You have to be there!*"

Sometimes, Off-the-Wall Wandas show their off-the-wall behavior in quieter, subtler ways. This is often more disconcerting because unlike the loud and obnoxious way of behaving, which is constant and predictable, the quiet, subtle behavior can catch a person off guard. Here are a couple of examples:

Wanda's son and DIL invite her over for dinner. It has been a long time since she has seen them, so they spend some time catching up on things. Wanda eventually goes into the family room to play with her grandchildren for a while. After about half an hour she comes back into the kitchen, where her DIL is preparing dinner. Within a few minutes, Wanda casually comments, "You know, it's not easy being a grandparent. You have no control over anything when it comes to your grandkids. You have to just sit back and trust that the people in charge know what they're doing." Wanda's DIL is stunned. She looks up, but she has no words.

or

Wanda's DIL is recuperating from minor surgery, so Wanda volunteers to bring over dinner. When she arrives at her son and DIL's house, she starts to put the food on the counter. Her DIL is in the kitchen with her. When Wanda pulls out the meat dish, her DIL is taken aback but is too shocked to say anything. Knowing full well that her DIL has an aversion to pork, Wanda had brought the one dish her DIL would not/could not eat.

Off-the-Wall Wanda's behavior also can appear to be subtle but manipulative. She may become withdrawn or sullen so that everyone becomes aware she's upset. This then causes everyone around her to try to fix things so she will return to her "less unpleasant" self. Another way Wanda may display this subtle, manipulative behavior is by pushing away the people she feels have wronged her. For example, during a family gathering she may ignore them or relegate them to a distant table or room where they are on the outside of things instead of being involved with everyone else. She may not even invite them to the gathering at all.

Uncertain Sara

At this point in her life, Uncertain Sara is pretty comfortable with who she is and comfortable in her own skin. However, she is less comfortable with who she is as a mother and MIL. These two roles – mother of an adult son and MIL to an adult woman – seem to come with no instruction manual and no clear examples for her to emulate.

Although Uncertain Sara feels emotionally that she has let go of her son, at times she finds interacting with him a bit challenging. She's experiencing new and different feelings that she doesn't understand, and her behavior often reflects those unsettled feelings. Sara wants to be part of her son and DIL's lives, and

49

yet she is not quite sure how that is supposed to happen. So she tries different things to make that connection, which cause her to behave in several different ways. And while she means well, these behaviors can make it difficult to feel comfortable and relaxed around her.

For example, Sara may at times continue in her mother role, trying to parent both her son and DIL, overstepping her bounds with what she says or what she does. And yet at other times, she keeps her distance to the degree that she appears more like a guest than a family member. She may act as though her priorities are a bit skewed – when her help is needed, she's oblivious to the request, but when her help is not really needed, she's almost suffocating. Uncertain Sara can come across a bit awkward when interacting with her DIL either because she tries too hard, she says strange things or she just does things that seem a bit off. For example:

> Sara knows her DIL likes to garden, but after the sixth gardening birthday gift in a row, her DIL says, *"Enough!"*

or

> Sara is at her son and DIL's house. As she walks around, she notices the silk plant in their foyer. She says out loud, not to anyone in particular, "You know, you can buy those cans of pressurized air that take dust right off these kinds of plants."

or

> Sara is buying gifts for the holidays. She buys her daughters the same scarf, but in different colors. She buys her DIL an ornate, antique gold-leaf picture frame. Her DIL's style is contemporary, and her home's décor reflects this contemporary style.

Although Uncertain Sara's actions are harmless, they can leave a person scratching his or her head wondering, *Did she really just say/do that?* Finally, Sara may act completely passive, as if waiting for her DIL to take the lead – yet giving no indication that this is what she is doing.

As you can see, these different MILs range from the "I am so lucky to have her in my life (or to be her)" type to the "I can't believe this is my life" variety. You may have found, as I mentioned at the start of this chapter, that different aspects of your behavior or your MIL's behavior fit into more than one of these types. That's actually pretty common. But when you take a step back, you will find more behaviors fit into one MIL type than into the others.

Now that we've identified the different MIL characters, it's time to take a closer look at the different DIL characters. Ready? Read on!

Chapter 4

Daughters-in-Law

Now we'll move on to the four basic types of daughter-in-law personalities, with stories and examples for each. As you did with the last chapter, see which type sounds the closest to the one in your relationship. You'll notice one difference, though, between this chapter on DILs and the last one dealing with the MIL characters. This chapter shows a strong connection between each DIL character and her relationship with her own mother. That's because the different DIL characters have developed into who they are in large part because of the relationship each DIL has had with her own mother (think about Chapter 2 and the topic of history and baggage). In other words, who the DIL is at this point is closely tied to the relationship she has had (or not had) with her own mother.

Ready to dive in? Great! First we'll discuss the preferred type, Confident Connie. Then we'll cover the more challenging types – Doubting Donna, Weird Wendy and Transitioned Tracy.

Confident Connie

Confident Connie is the DIL that every MIL dreams of having. She has a good, comfortable sense of who she is, and she's emotionally independent from her mother. Specifically, her strong sense of who she is comes from feeling like a grown-up. It comes from trusting herself, her thoughts and her opinions. It comes from liking who she is and seeing herself as others see her.

Because Connie has such a strong sense of herself, she stays consistent in her thoughts, her beliefs and her behavior – regardless of who is around or what the situation is. And yet Connie isn't rigid by any means. Instead, she's open to hearing what others have to say and is relaxed about their input; she's not threatened by another person's point of view. For example:

> Connie's close friend Rachel makes a comment about Connie's decision to switch her daughter from one soccer club to another. The way Rachel says it implies that she thinks Connie is either making a mistake, being selfish or at least not thinking things through. Connie hears her friend out, and she is really OK with what Rachel says even though she doesn't agree with her friend. Connie doesn't feel that she needs to defend her choice, nor does she start to doubt that making the switch was the right thing to do for her daughter. Connie knows who she is and trusts that she made a good, solid decision based on what she knew at the time.

Because Confident Connie is emotionally independent from her own mother, that healthy separation allows her to gain strength in who she is. That doesn't necessarily mean that her mother no longer affects her. (We'll describe that situation a bit further on in this chapter.) What it *does* mean is that as Connie has developed a stronger sense of

herself, her mother's influence has become less dominant. Connie can let her mother be who her mother is *without* Connie feeling as though she has to change who *she* is. This allows Connie to feel comfortable and confident in who she is as a young woman.

Confident Connie's ability to emotionally separate from her mother and develop a strong sense of herself can mean one of two things. It can mean that the relationship Connie has with her mother is a healthy, supportive relationship based on mutual respect, or it can mean that the relationship is limited or even nonexistent, due to a subtle or not-so-subtle push-pull, emotionally charged quality that appears early on in the relationship.

In the first scenario – where the relationship is a healthy, supportive one – Connie's mother gave Connie opportunities to express herself as she was growing up as well as opportunities to make choices and decisions on her own. Her mother supported her and helped her build the confidence she needed to trust herself. This  allowed Connie to develop her own thoughts, feelings and beliefs – even if they were different from those her mother had. As a result, by the time Connie reached adulthood, both Connie and her mother had developed a respectful appreciation for each other as women.

This doesn't mean that Confident Connie and her mother always get along or agree on everything. It means that they both recognize their differences and for the most part don't let those differences get in the way of their relationship. When they do disagree, Connie and her mother pick and choose their battles. Connie feels as though she can speak up if she chooses, her mother will listen to what she thinks, and she is able to resolve things with her mother or at least clear the air.

In the second scenario – where there was a subtle or not-so-subtle push-pull, emotionally charged relationship early on – things get a bit more complex. For example:

At 7 years old, Connie is so excited about her upcoming dance recital she can hardly stand it. She's talked nonstop to anyone who would listen to her chatter on about it. She's been practicing for months, and finally, the show is tomorrow. After dinner, Connie goes into her room and starts practicing her dance. Her mother comes to her bedroom door and says, "I won't be able to go to the recital. Why don't you see if you can get a ride with your friend Jane?" Her mother then turns away and walks down the hall.

At 13, Connie walks in the door after spending the night at a friend's house. She sees her mother sitting in the chair, staring out the window. She tries talking to her mother, but her mother responds with one-word answers in a tone Connie knows only too well. Although Connie isn't sure why her mother is acting this way, she's aware this is another "bad day" for her mother. Without thinking, Connie begins picking up the clutter in the living room, emptying the dishwasher and checking on her younger brother and sister to be sure they are playing quietly in the other part of the house.

In this type of mother-daughter relationship, Connie eventually was able to come to terms with the fact that her mother was not capable of being there for her emotionally or sometimes even physically. She learned to depend on herself and on others to get her needs met. Unlike in the first scenario (where Connie develops a strong sense of herself through her mother's support and love), here Confident Connie is able to develop a strong sense of herself because her mother's emotional or physical absence has required it.

Usually, one of two different types of mothers creates this situation: either a mother who is more focused on herself and her own needs than she is on those of her daughter (as in the first example above) or a mother who has difficulty feeling like a grown-up emotionally and who struggles with being the mom because she feels needy herself and wants to be taken care of (as in the second example). Neither of these possibilities leaves much room for a healthy mother-daughter relationship. *The bond may be there, but the relationship is not.*

In both of these cases, Connie learns that she needs to depend on herself more than she depends on her mother. The first type of mother gives little or no thought to Connie's needs, yet she expects Connie to understand and accept that *she* has needs. In addition, regardless of Connie's age, she typically views Connie as being able to take care of herself.

The second type of mother can go from being OK to suddenly appearing emotionally fragile and vulnerable with little warning. This type of mother sends out a "take care of me" vibe, putting Confident Connie in the position of feeling as though it is her job to make sure her mother is all right. The unspoken rule is that taking care of her mother is the way Connie can show her mother that she loves her. If that rule is ever broken, Connie's mother becomes emotionally distant and often "goes away" for hours or days, leaving Connie to fend for herself emotionally and sometimes even physically.

Regardless of *how* Connie became a confident, independent woman (whether through a close or a distant relationship with her own mother), the fact that Connie knows herself well and is comfortable with who she is makes it easy for her to see her MIL for who *she* really is.

Doubting Donna

Unlike Confident Connie, Doubting Donna is not really comfortable with who she is. She tends to second-guess her thoughts, feelings and actions and is more often than not judgmental and self-critical. Donna is struggling with her sense of self because this is what she learned growing up.

As a freshman in high school, Donna wins a high-achievement award. She receives a plaque, and a picture of her with the school officials and the winners from the other three grades appears in the paper. Donna's mother tells her how proud she is of her, but then she quietly adds, "Oh, I wish you had worn the blue dress I bought you."

These conflicting messages Doubting Donna receives from her mother teach her to criticize herself and doubt herself. Instead of being proud of her accomplishments, Donna begins focusing on why she hadn't known the right dress to wear – something she feels she somehow should have been aware of. Just as important, she is also upset with herself because she let her mother down. In the end, whatever positive feelings Donna's accomplishments give her are negated by her mother's actions.

On the surface, the relationship between Doubting Donna and her mother can appear quite close and sometimes even loving, yet there's an undercurrent of tension, yearning and strife. As all children do, Donna looks to her mother for acceptance and encouragement to help her feel loved and valued, which helps create a strong sense of self. Donna loves her mother and wants to please her mother so she can feel her mother's love. However, her mother gives her confusing, mixed messages. As a result, Donna is always chasing after that *one* indication, that *one* expression, word or action from her mother that lets her know she matters. Unfortunately, Doubting Donna never really gets it.

Despite the fact that Donna loves her mother, she struggles throughout her life with these unsettling feelings of frustration, hurt and anger that always seem to be just under the surface. This is not something that she can point to and say, "This is what I'm feeling. This is what is going on." Rather, this is something she feels deep down inside. The struggle – both with her mother and with her own self-doubt and uncertainty – may affect Donna long into adulthood. For example:

> Donna and her husband just bought a new house. They are out of their starter home and living in a house that clearly represents who they are and where they're going. Donna is excited because more than anything this house symbolizes the fact that she is now a "grown-up." She just can't stop talking about it. The first thing she wants to do is tell her mother the fabulous news. As soon as she can, she calls her mother and invites her over. Her

mother expresses excitement, as well, and plans a time to come to their new house.

The time arrives, and Donna's mother is late – not just a few minutes late, but half an hour late. When she gets there, she immediately comments on how hard the house was to find. Donna is hurt, but she thinks to herself, *It doesn't matter. She's here, and now I can show her the house – my house.* She and her mother go inside. Her mother walks around without saying anything for what feels like an hour. Finally she speaks, "Huh … This is certainly an interesting layout." She walks around a bit more and then says, "What do you plan to do with this odd little space here?" – at which point Donna feels her whole body wilt.

Here's another example:

Donna's mother mentions to Donna that she'd like both Donna and her husband to attend a particular family event. As soon as her mother starts talking about the event, Donna begins to feel a bit anxious. It's not something Donna really wants to do because it would require rearranging her own plans, inconveniencing her husband and adding more work to their already busy schedules. Donna timidly says something to this effect. Her comment is met with silence. Then her mother mentions that it's important to the family that Donna and her husband be there. Within milliseconds, Donna begins to convince herself that she can easily do this. *It's no big deal,* she thinks. *I'd really like to see the family anyway.* She tells her husband that they should go just this one time. Although it causes an argument between the two of them, Donna makes it happen. She and her husband attend the family event.

As these examples show, Doubting Donna's mother can still affect how Donna feels and maybe even what she does. She has mixed feelings about her mother that are often but not always buried underneath the love she feels. This unresolved struggle and the doubt that ultimately results about what she wants for herself end up clouding how Donna perceives herself as well as how she perceives other people and their actions. This "perceptive cloudiness" can then cause Donna to be hypersensitive to someone challenging her, questioning her or even just feeling differently than the way she does. And when this hypersensitivity swings into high gear, Donna tends to feel defensive, which then shows in her words and actions. Here's an example:

Donna is sitting on the couch trying to read, but she feels distracted. Her husband is at the table, reading the paper. Donna's fidgeting catches his attention, and he turns to her and asks, "What's going on? You all right?"

Trying to keep her cool but finding that hard to maintain, Donna blurts out, "Why does she have to be like that?"

"She who?" he responds, confused.

Exasperated, Donna raises her voice a bit and answers, *"Your mother!"*

Dreading what is about to come next, but knowing he has to stay with this, her husband asks, "What are you talking about? What did she do?"

"What she always does! She always takes over. Like her thoughts and opinions are the only ones that matter. She treats me like a child."

Her husband is starting to feel sick inside. He really hates this. He doesn't know what to do, but he feels he has to fix it. "Tell me what she did."

Donna begins gearing up. "Where do I begin? She was over here earlier today helping me plan for the holidays – if 'help' is what you want to call it. Every time I brought up something I wanted to do, she had to say why that wasn't a good idea. Then she'd tell me what I *should* do, which totally ticked me off ... ."

"So did you say something to her?"

Feeling even more frustrated, Donna raises her voice further. "Of course I didn't! You know how your mother is. Why does she have to be like that? I should be able to do what I want to."

Her husband tries to interject, but by now, Donna's on a roll.

As you can see, the undercurrent of Doubting Donna's emotional struggle with her own mother greatly affects not only how Donna sees herself, but also how she sees her MIL. Donna's clouds of doubt, uncertainty and personal discomfort leave her feeling challenged by as well as disregarded by her MIL. So even an innocent gesture from her MIL can set into motion Donna's feelings of being judged or criticized.

Weird Wendy

Weird Wendy has a completely different style. She has little or no desire to engage with most people, so she comes across as distant and aloof. When Wendy does interact with someone, particularly when she's talking with friends, her own family or her husband's family, she often perceives them through distorted filters, creating confusion, tension and misunderstandings. Then she digs her heels in, not allowing herself to even consider another point of view. She believes her perspective is the only one that's real. Here's an example:

Wendy receives a call from her MIL inviting Wendy and her husband to an out-of-town birthday party for her husband's grandmother, who is turning 85. Her MIL talks a little about the upcoming event, letting Wendy know that the gathering will be a semiformal affair. She also mentions that the couple is welcome to stay at her house, or if they prefer, she will pay for a hotel room. As Wendy listens, she starts to fume. She feels manipulated and pressured by her MIL. Trying hard to keep her cool, Wendy mumbles quickly, "OK, let me get back to you," and then gets off the phone as soon as she can.

What would make Weird Wendy perceive her MIL as pushy and manipulative, particularly when this is so far from reality? Usually it involves two emotions – feelings of anxiety and entitlement – not to mention having a complicated relationship with her own mother. Wendy's mother can behave in two extremely different ways toward her, and each results in Wendy having a distorted view of other people's behavior. Either she can coddle, overprotect and infantilize Wendy, or she can put Wendy in a position where Wendy feels she needs to take care of her mother instead of her mother taking care of Wendy. Either situation creates a sense of entitlement in Wendy. It's easy to grasp how the first way – coddling, overprotecting and infantilizing – can instill a sense of entitlement in someone. But it's less clear how that works with the second scenario, where Weird Wendy feels she has to take care of her mother. Let me touch on both.

If her mother does everything for Wendy as she's growing up, not to mention well into Wendy's adulthood, Wendy will find it difficult to learn how to take care of herself. She will never learn how to figure things out, solve problems or work through difficult times. If she's never really been allowed to see how she can be successful at achieving something on her own then she will have unrealistic expectations of the people around her, including her husband, family, in-laws and the few friends she may have.

On the flip side, if Weird Wendy is the one who, as a child, takes care of her mother and possibly even her siblings, she will then feel entitled – not because she doesn't know how to take care of herself but

I CAN'T. I NEED TO STAY HERE. MY MOM'S IN ONE OF 'HER MOODS' AGAIN.

because she feels she never had the chance to be a child – to have someone take care of her. She will feel resentful and angry, yet she may not even be aware of these feelings.

In either of these circumstances, Weird Wendy feels that no one sees her, hears her or recognizes her needs. And so either way, Wendy becomes hypersensitive to anyone asking something of her. Even when someone is just having a casual conversation with Wendy, she has a tendency to feel as though the person wants something from her, and as a result she feels suspicious and resentful.

Along with feeling entitled, Wendy also experiences a high degree of anxiety. She's often so anxious and so afraid that she can't think or act outside of her narrow comfort zone. To do so would create too much anxiety, too much fear. The combination of Weird Wendy's hypersensitivity to what others say or do, her feelings of entitlement and her high degree of anxiety often makes her behavior seem extremely selfish, with everything needing to be about her.

So how does this relate to Wendy's relationship with her MIL? Thanks to Wendy's sense of entitlement and her anxiety, Wendy puts all of her MIL's actions under a microscope, scrutinizing everything her MIL says or does. Wendy is then likely to perceive her MIL's actions as attempts to take something tangible or emotional away from her, which puts Wendy in a hyper-protective mode. Wendy puts up defenses so as not to let her MIL get anywhere near her emotionally for fear that her MIL will take something from her – just as her own mother did.

Transitioned Tracy

Transitioned Tracy, on the other hand, has worked through some of the earlier issues she had with her mother. As a result, Tracy is at a point in her life where she feels more comfortable with herself, proud of what she's accomplished and fairly self-contained. Because of the inner work she's done on herself, Transitioned Tracy has grown into her own and developed a better sense of who she is. She's autonomous and independent, and she doesn't feel the need to rely on others unless absolutely necessary. In her relationships, she operates from a position of strength and is careful in choosing with whom she is vulnerable – and her MIL is *not* one of those people. Tracy is not really interested in building a relationship with her. For example:

Tracy and her MIL are spending the afternoon together while Tracy's husband helps his father with repairs around the house. Tracy has nothing against her MIL, but she finds it difficult to be around her at times. While Tracy is sitting on the couch reading a book, her MIL is sorting through some old pictures.

"Have you seen these pictures of when the kids were all babies?" she says to her DIL. "They were so adorable. You know, none of them has really changed a bit."

Only half listening, Tracy mumbles, "Uh-huh."

Without looking up, her MIL continues, "I've looked at these a thousand times. I never get tired of looking at them. Our family has always been so close."

Tracy glances up from her book with a puzzled look on her face. She knows this isn't true. Her husband has told her stories about what it was like for him growing up, and the picture he painted wasn't of family closeness. Tracy starts to say something but stops herself. *It's really not worth it to say anything,* she thinks as she goes back to reading.

After a while, her MIL looks up and says, "It must have been hard growing up in a divorced home … going from your mom's house to your dad's all the time."

Tracy doesn't want to have this conversation with her MIL. They aren't close. It feels intrusive. Tracy decides to get away from the conversation and away from her MIL – at least for a while. Tracy closes her book and gets up from the couch, saying, "You know, I think I'll go for a walk. I'll be back in a little while."

As you can see, Transitioned Tracy doesn't want to share things with her MIL. She doesn't dislike her, but she doesn't feel particularly close to her either. To understand Tracy better, we need to look at her relationship with her own mother. She may have had one of two different types of relationships.

Transitioned Tracy's relationship with her own mother may have started out like the relationship Doubting Donna has with her mother (who continually gave her daughter mixed messages when she was growing up, leaving her feeling unsure of her own thoughts and feelings and resulting in her daughter feeling bad about herself most of the time). Although both struggled for quite some time in their mother-daughter relationship, the difference between Tracy and Donna is that Tracy eventually worked through many of her issues and now feels pretty good about herself. (Tracy's mother, however, may or may not have worked through these same issues – and if she hasn't, her relationship with Tracy could be strained.)

On the other hand, Transitioned Tracy's relationship with her mother may be more like the relationship Confident Connie has with her mother. Her childhood years may have been good, with Tracy experiencing a healthy balance between feeling mothered and being encouraged to be independent. The relationship both Tracy and Connie have with their mothers is built on a strong, loving foundation that never wavered, but as time has marched on, Tracy's hit a few bumps. Maybe Tracy had a stormy adolescence or maybe something major in her mother's life changed – or both. Even so, their solid foundation has allowed Transitioned Tracy to regain the closeness she once had with her mother.

No matter how Tracy transitioned into the woman she is today, she is not looking for another mother in her MIL. Tracy sees herself on equal footing with her MIL rather than seeing herself as someone looking for guidance or direction from her in-law.

Just as with the last chapter, the different relationships presented here range from the ideal to the "Get real!" You've probably identified familiar traits in more than one of these types – but one usually predominates over the others. If the description that resonates the most leaves you feeling less than optimistic about your relationship, hang in there. You're about to see how you can turn it around for the better.

Chapter 5

Husbands and Sons

Before we jump into the different husband/son patterns, let's look at a man's relationship with his mother. It starts, of course, in childhood. All children – boys and girls included – need the love, nurturance and support of their mothers. They need to feel their mothers' love and be able to depend on their mothers physically, emotionally and psychologically. Children learn to trust that Mom is the one place where they can go to feel safe, to feel unbroken and to feel whole regardless of what is going on in the world around them. A child needs to feel this in order to grow, flourish and survive.

For boys to become healthy adults, however, they need to be able to survive life's roadblocks and crises on their own from a place that feels safe and whole, a place similar to the one they had with their mother, but one they now find within themselves. In this inner sanctum, the man must be the one who is in control – not his mother, and not his wife. He needs to figure out how to create this place within himself and how to trust himself from within it. For this to occur, men need not only to separate from their mothers but also to become distinct from them.

This chapter presents the three basic types of husband/son personalities, each reflecting a different degree of transition into adulthood. First, we'll look at confident Self-Assured Andy, the preferred type. As we move on to In-the-Middle Michael and Struggling Steven, you will get a clear picture of which personality type best fits your husband or son, based on the examples, stories and descriptions of the way each type handles (or doesn't handle) particular situations with mothers and wives.

By now, you won't be surprised to hear that you may find that your husband or son has characteristics that fall into one or more of the different categories, depending on the situation. Rest assured that this is not uncommon and that upon further reflection, you will find that one of the descriptions fits him more often than do the others.

Self-Assured Andy

Because he has become emotionally independent of his mother, Self-Assured Andy is self-confident and has a strong sense of who he is as a man. He stands firm in his beliefs and is comfortable with his role in life. He is also clear about his priorities and where everyone fits within them – including his wife, his mother and himself.

As he grew from boy to man, Andy made a healthy transition into adulthood, creating a place within where he trusts himself, believes in himself and feels grounded, safe and whole. The relationship he currently has with his mother is forever different from the one he had with her when he was a child. Now, he sees her as someone who is more than a mother, and he sees himself as an adult who is on equal footing with her. Because of this, Self-Assured Andy has established healthy boundaries with his mother and puts her opinions and behaviors in perspective. For example:

Andy's mother has some concerns about several comments his wife has made to her. She's not sure if she should say something to her DIL or if she should just act as though nothing happened – even though she can't get the younger woman's remarks out of her head. Deciding to discuss the matter with her son, she starts by saying, "Andy, I need to talk to you about a conversation I had with Connie last week."

"Mom, I know where you are going with this," Andy responds before she has a chance to continue. "I love you," he adds, thoughtfully and lovingly, "but I'm not going to talk to you about it. I will talk to you about anything but Connie."

Depending on his mother's ability to grow beyond her role as mother or to have the ability or willingness to be self-reflective, Self-Assured Andy either roots his current relationship with her in a healthy balance of closeness and separation, or he determines that it is best to maintain some distance from her.

In-the-Middle Michael

Unlike Self-Assured Andy, In-the-Middle Michael feels caught in between his wife and his mother. He is not sure how to balance his relationship with each of them or where everyone fits in his new world as a man. He may or may not have separated from his mother, but he definitely hasn't finished becoming distinct from her. He has not yet completed the journey of finding that place within himself where he is safe and whole. Although he may feel this place at times and know theoretically that it is indeed there, this feeling is not consistent enough for him to trust himself from within that place.

Because In-the-Middle Michael is still trying to find his footing as a man, he struggles to please too many people with little or no thought about what makes sense to *him*. Because he sees himself as the common denominator between his wife and mother, he will attempt either to be the mediator between them or to stay away from the issues they have with each other in hopes that they will resolve the problems on their own. For example:

Michael can see that his wife is upset about his mother's response to their wanting to put the kids in a summer camp program. He knows his mother meant well, so he attempts to clarify her words by saying, "She didn't mean it like that," or "She was just suggesting ...," hoping this will make his wife less angry. It's not the only time he's played go-between. Just last week, his mother made a comment about his wife snubbing her when she mentioned she was thinking about coming over. Michael was not sure what his mother wanted him to say, so he tried to give an explanation for his wife's behavior by saying things like, "You just caught her at a bad time" and "I'm sure you're reading it wrong," hoping to soothe his mother's hurt feelings.

or

Michael's wife is angry that his mother has come into their house to drop something off when they weren't home. When she tries to talk to him about it, he just shrugs and says, "What's the big deal? I don't know why you're so upset. If it bothers you so much, say something to her." This isn't the only time he's tried to avoid what was going on between them. The other day, his mother was telling him how upset she was with the way his wife spoke to her. She felt it was rude and disrespectful. Although Michael was present during that conversation, he responded to his mother's complaints by saying, "Really? I don't remember." When his mother pressed the point, he commented, "She said that? I didn't hear it."

In-the-Middle Michael's behavior as a middleman affects his relationship with both his mother and his wife. He may act like a little boy when he is around his mother, only to cause more problems with his wife. Or he may become distant, anxious or uncommunicative with his mother, which encourages her to cling to him even more. With his wife, Michael becomes mute when she tries to discuss his mother with him, which only makes her even angrier.

Any of these scenarios creates more fighting between Michael and his wife, as she begins to view her husband differently – respecting and trusting him less. Remember the example above about In-the-Middle Michael's wife being upset because her MIL came into their house when they weren't home? Here's what happens the next time that situation occurs:

Michael and his wife have just walked into their house when they see two bags of fresh fruits and vegetables, some coupon clippings and their newspaper on the counter. His wife rolls her eyes and groans, "She was here, wasn't she?"

"Apparently," Michael answers.

"Why does she have to do that – come into our house without even calling first to see if we're here?"

Michael hears his wife's frustration, but he doesn't really see what the big deal is. After all, they had given his mother a key to their house when they first bought it. It was as much his wife's idea as it was his. Michael doesn't know what to say. He decides to say nothing, hoping the conversation will just end.

Realizing that Michael is not responding to her, his wife becomes even more upset. "Doesn't it bother you?" she asks insistently.

"Not really, I guess," Michael says with a shrug, starting to take the fruit out of the bag.

Feeling even more annoyed because it's clear Michael just doesn't get it, his wife raises her voice. "*I can't believe you!*" she exclaims. "How many times have I told you that I *hate* it when she just comes into our house? You really ought to say something to your mom. It's *our* house, and she needs to respect that!"

Michael continues emptying the bags, waiting for his wife to finish, saying nothing because he's not sure what to say.

"Can't you say *something*?" she asks, now totally exasperated.

"What do you want me to say?" Michael responds, feeling trapped.

At this point his wife shakes her head in utter disbelief, thinking, *He just doesn't get it!*

Struggling Steven

Unlike In-the-Middle Michael, Struggling Steven has managed to separate from (and for the most part has become distinct from) his mother. He is fairly OK with who he is, but not completely. He likes some things about himself, but he's not entirely comfortable or confident. Steven tends to over-think, over-worry and over-analyze his actions and their impact on other people. Yet all his turmoil is internal. Outwardly, he appears oblivious to many of the stresses in his life. When people see him, they think he's just fine when in reality he is silently ruminating and fretting about things over which he has no control.

Struggling Steven knows his wife doesn't particularly like his family, but he isn't sure why. He knows various family members have made some mistakes along the way but nothing that would warrant the way his wife treats them. He sees his mother trying to reach out to his wife, only to receive a lukewarm or downright cool response. And his wife can't really give him an explanation for her behavior that makes sense. So although Steven feels anxious about the situation, he does nothing, says nothing and hopes it will change. Instead of stepping in to fix it the way In-the-Middle Michael would, Struggling Steven deliberately avoids what he sees occurring between them because he doesn't really know how to deal with their problem without creating more of a problem for *him*. For example:

> Steven and his wife are at his parents' house for a small family get-together. When they arrive, Steven makes the rounds, briefly greeting everyone. After Steven spends some time talking with different family members, someone asks him where his wife is. When he doesn't see her, he thinks she must have left the room for a minute or so. But time passes, and she doesn't return. He starts getting a sick feeling in his stomach. More time passes, and she still doesn't return. Although no one says anything, Steven feels the awkwardness in the room growing. He doesn't know how to respond. Finally, he leaves the room in search of his wife. He finds her in the den, reading a magazine. He doesn't know what to do or what to say – to her, or to his family.

Struggling Steven wants his wife to be happy. She's not. He wants her to get along with his family. She doesn't. But he has no idea what to do to change the situation. What often happens is that Steven creates fewer and fewer instances requiring his wife to interact with his family. He may agree to avoid some of his family's more casual gatherings with the understanding that his wife will agree to accompany him to the bigger, more traditional events. He hopes this compromise will encourage his wife to be less aloof and distant when they are all together. It rarely works, if ever.

You have probably recognized that Self-Assured Andy, In-the-Middle Michael and Struggling Steven range from one end of the spectrum to the other in terms of the way they deal with the relationships between their wives and mothers. Some of you may be concerned that "Once a Michael, always a Michael" or wonder, "Is there any hope for Struggling Steven?" I am here to assure you that there is indeed hope for both. Neither a Michael nor a Steven has to remain as he is.

The Characters

Mothers-in-Law

Comfortable Carla

 She has created a new identity for herself beyond that of "mother." She is clear that her new role in her son's life is secondary to his wife's role.

Mothering Margaret

 She struggles with letting go of her mom role. She wants things to be as they have always been, even though circumstances are now different.

Off-the-Wall Wanda

 She comes across as mean, insensitive and self-centered. Everything is about her and what she feels, wants and needs. Her behavior is often extreme in nature.

Uncertain Sara

 She has let go of her son, but she is uncertain about her new role as a mother to an adult child and to a DIL. Sometimes she tries too hard, and sometimes she just misses the mark.

Daughters-in-Law

Confident Connie

She has a strong sense of who she is. She trusts herself, her thoughts and her opinions. She likes who she is and sees herself as others see her.

Doubting Donna

She is not comfortable with who she is. She tends to second-guess her thoughts, feelings and actions. More often than not, she is judgmental and self-critical.

Weird Wendy

She has little or no desire to engage with most people. As a result, she comes across as distant and aloof. She typically perceives any friends, family or in-laws through distorted filters.

Transitioned Tracy

She has worked through earlier issues she had with her mother. She now feels comfortable with who she is and is fairly self-contained. She is independent and does not rely on others.

Husbands/Sons

Self-Assured Andy

 He is self-confident with a strong sense of who he is as a man. He stands firm on his beliefs and is comfortable with his role in life. He has established healthy boundaries with his mother.

In-the-Middle Michael

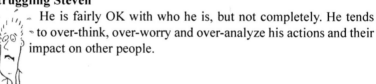 He feels caught in the middle between his wife and mother. He is not sure how to balance his relationship with each of them or where everyone fits in his new world as a man.

Struggling Steven

He is fairly OK with who he is, but not completely. He tends to over-think, over-worry and over-analyze his actions and their impact on other people.

Part III:

Patterns and Solutions

Introduction to the Patterns and Solutions

Now that you've been introduced to the characters and have some idea which ones best fit you, your in-law and your husband or son, it's time to see how those personalities come together in a particular behavior pattern – and how best to negotiate that pattern. Chapter 6 presents descriptions of the four MIL-DIL behavior patterns – the Camelot pattern, the Walking on Eggshells pattern, the Does She Seem Nuts to You? pattern and the It Is ... What It Is pattern.

In my more than 30 years working as a mental-health professional, I've seen these patterns numerous times. I can assure you, people do not find each other and marry by chance. Many subtle and not-so-subtle influences play into our choice of mates, influences that go way beyond the simple "we love each other and want to spend our lives together" reasoning. These undercurrents operate in *all* our relationships, including friendships as well as marriages and extended families. The difference is that friendships have limitations that marriages and extended families do not – and this is where it can get complicated.

As you read the descriptions of these different patterns, you may find that your relationship dynamic seems to fit into more than one pattern (just as you may have found in Part II that you or your in-law fit into more than one character description). Don't be confused – this is not that unusual.

Remember that as we experience life, each of us is always growing, changing and evolving. We all go through major (and minor) life events that affect us and change who we are – and this then affects how we perceive and relate to the people around us. (For example, my DIL Michelle and I got along really well in the early years of our relationship. It wasn't until she had her first child that things between us started to go awry.)

After you have identified your particular relationship pattern, it'll be time for you to roll up your sleeves and get to work. To help you begin to make the shift necessary for real change, Chapter 7 will help you look at how your in-law might be perceiving your words or behavior – which is often quite different from what you had intended – as well as how your reactions to your MIL or DIL can affect how your in-law then responds to you. I've included some exercises that will really bring this concept home. The perception discussion and the reaction discussion will each offer two separate exercises – one for MILs and one for DILs – so that you can maintain the focus on your specific in-law.

Part III ends with a discussion of specific solutions or tools – Chapters 8, 9 and 10 designed specifically for MILs and Chapters 11, 12 and 13 designed expressly for DILs – that can make interactions with your particular in-law work more smoothly. Rest assured that through-out my many years of clinical practice teaching numerous clients to use these tools, what I found was that *these tools work*. I've seen women experience their relationships improving in ways that they could only dream about before.

But to make these extraordinary changes, you must practice them, fine-tune them to your particular situation, adapt them as needed and keep using them. Remember to be patient – don't expect perfection on your first few tries. Success requires approaching this work with a genuine commitment to doing whatever it takes to make this relationship work for you *and* your in-law. Keep in mind that the goal is not to be right but to strengthen the relationship.

Chapter 6

Patterns

This chapter will introduce the four different patterns that exist in the MIL-DIL relationship dynamic. You'll find that one of them (either Camelot, Walking on Eggshells, Does She Seem Nuts to You? or It Is … What It Is) is the one that best fits you and your in-law.

As you read this chapter, you'll notice that not every conceivable combination of characters is covered. For example, you won't find a pattern that shows Mothering Margaret having raised Self-Assured Andy or Doubting Donna married to Struggling Steven. That's because all the mathematically possible outcomes just aren't represented in real life. In all my years of clinical practice, and in all the case studies I examined in my research, only these four patterns (covered in a total of seven possible character combinations) occur.

This isn't really all that surprising if you consider two general principles. First, we are a product of our parents. So a Mothering Margaret would be too much of a "take-charge" kind of mother for her son to turn out to be a Self-Assured Andy (who can separate from his mother more easily and cleanly). Second, the mates we are most drawn to and those we are most likely to find ourselves in a relationship with are those who feel emotionally familiar to us (whether that familiarity has positive associations or negative ones). You've heard the expression that we all marry either our mothers or our fathers? Well, it's quite often true. And this is what that is referring to. Whether we realize it consciously or not, it's human nature for us to seek what feels familiar and so to recreate the relationships that we emotionally already know when we pick a partner and start a new family. We don't fall into relationships randomly.

As you read the descriptions of the patterns outlined here, you'll discover how the perceptions and reactions of the different characters within each specific pattern come together not only to form the unique qualities of that pattern, but also to help create the characteristics of the individuals themselves. Keep in mind, however, that just because you identify with one pattern now doesn't mean you'll remain that way forever. People grow and change all the time. As you evolve throughout your life, you may find you perceive other people and situations differently and therefore react differently than you would have in the past. So you may want to revisit this chapter a few years from now and see where you are then. Now, let's get started!

Camelot

When you bring Comfortable Carla, Self-Assured Andy and Confident Connie together you have Camelot. This is a healthy, comfortable, drama-free relationship. But it doesn't happen by magic. It happens because all three individuals involved understand their own roles as well as each of the others' roles in this new family dynamic. And they all respect the boundaries inherent in their relationships.

Comfortable Carla has let go of her son, Self-Assured Andy, and has created a new identity for herself that is more than just being her son's mom. She has no hidden agenda, no need to be needed and no misperceptions of who her DIL, Confident Connie, is. Not only does Carla love Connie because Connie loves Carla's son, but she also loves Connie for the qualities that make Connie who she is. Even if Carla and Connie don't always agree, Carla respects the choices that her son and DIL make. She appreciates their need to be the adults they want to be. Because of Carla's ability to move past her role as a mother, she is able to perceive Connie's words and behaviors for what they are and react accordingly, creating a smooth and easy flow in the relationship.

For his part, Self-Assured Andy has not only separated from his mother, but he has become distinct from her as well. He is comfortable with who he is as a man and is clear on which relationship has priority in his life – the one he has with his wife, Confident Connie. And it shows in his behavior.

Because of this, Connie feels secure in her relationship with Andy and knows they are aligned, making their relationship a strong, solid union. Connie's strong sense of herself and confidence in who she is helps her perceive Comfortable Carla for who Carla is – Andy's mother. Connie doesn't feel threatened, intimidated or even frustrated with Carla because she feels the respect Carla gives to her and to the boundaries Connie sets with Carla. If Carla occasionally says or does something out of bounds, Connie sees it for what it is (Carla being human), and she makes no undue judgment or criticism.

When you have three distinct individuals who respect each other, accept their respective roles and honor each other's boundaries, Camelot is bound to happen.

Walking on Eggshells

Walking on Eggshells feels entirely different. All three people in this relationship (Mothering Margaret, Doubting Donna and In-the-Middle Michael) are struggling. They struggle not only with who they are, but also with how they perceive the others in this relationship. It seems that everyone is looking at someone else and pointing fingers, not really seeing or acknowledging his or her own part in what is going on. Consequently, their relationships with one another are riddled with pain and difficulty.

Mothering Margaret's major challenge in this pattern is that she can't seem to completely let go of her "mom" role. And because of this, she perceives her DIL, Doubting Donna, as the one who "took her son away." This perception of Donna just builds on Margaret's fear that she will lose her son altogether and that the emotional connection she has always had with him will be broken. She's afraid her son will choose to shift his emotional alliance to Donna and away from her. And although that is what *should* happen in a healthy relationship, Mothering Margaret cannot see that this is a natural part of *any* marriage, let alone of her son's marriage. And as a result, Margaret feels so much loss, anger and fear that these emotions often cloud how she views the actions of her DIL. She's quick to feel left out, misunderstood and even competitive.

However, there is another side to Margaret's feelings. Mothering Margaret really wants to get along with Doubting Donna, and deep down inside Margaret may even like her (or at least she did like her at one time). It's just hard for Margaret to let any of these positive feelings be in the forefront when all the fear and anxiety she has about losing her son seem to take over. As a result, Margaret bounces between feelings of wanting a relationship with her DIL, blaming her for taking her son away and writhing in the agony of losing her emotional connection with her son. For example:

> Margaret is excited when she hears that her DIL, Donna, is planning a party for Donna's husband. Although Margaret and Donna don't always get along, it seems at the moment they are enjoying the discussion about the party. Margaret wants to help, and she waits, hoping Donna will ask her to help out in some way. When this doesn't happen, Margaret initially feels hurt, but then she decides to volunteer to help. She mentions her willingness to Donna, but Donna appears to be a little hesitant to respond. Margaret feels snubbed. She thinks that Donna doesn't want her help but won't say anything to her about it. At this moment, Margaret is not sure what to do. She knows if she says something, it could cause a war between her and Donna; but if she says nothing, she knows these feelings of hurt and anger will just stay with her. She's caught up in knots wanting to say something but feeling fearful to do so. And although she indeed ends up saying nothing, her bottled-up hurt and anger come out in her behavior.

For his part, In-the-Middle Michael is really at a loss. He's so unsure of himself, his role as a man, his role as a husband and his role as a son that he doesn't know where one role ends and another begins. Instead of standing firm on what *he* believes and trusting that what he thinks is valid and true for him, he just wants everyone to be happy. Consequently, his behavior reflects both his uncertainty in his different roles and his unrealistic desire that everyone should magically just get along. Because of his own internal confusion and angst, Michael reacts with frustration and sometimes even with anger toward his wife for (in his view) being the one responsible for making his life so much harder. (Michael doesn't blame his mother, however, and if he ever were to feel anger toward his mother for some reason, he would never dare express it.) Here's an example:

Michael is listening to his wife complain about his mother. She has been going on non-stop for about 20 minutes. He can see both his wife's side and his mother's side, so he tries to make a point here and there, hoping that he can help his wife see another way to look at things. Not only do his words seem to fall on deaf ears, but also his wife appears to be getting even angrier. Finally, frustrated and tired of his wife ignoring his attempts to talk to her, Michael says to his wife, "If you don't like it, say something to her. What do you want from me, anyway?" This does not exactly go over very well and only makes the situation worse.

Then there's Doubting Donna, who is always second-guessing herself. When she does manage to make a decision, she can't hear anything contrary about it without becoming defensive. Because of her doubts and self-questioning, Donna often feels anxious, just waiting to hear if what she's said or done is going to be accepted by the people that matter to her. And in spite of how it appears on the outside, her MIL *does* matter. She may not exactly want to be *friends* with her MIL or she may, but either way Donna wants her MIL to see her as a capable, adult woman. Yet Donna often feels she's not treated with respect by her MIL, and so whenever Donna is around Mothering Margaret, she becomes anxious and hyper-sensitive, anticipating this disrespect and gearing up for any bad attitudes that may come her way. Donna also questions her husband's loyalty. To her, it seems he doesn't take her side whenever his mother is involved. For example:

> Donna is talking to her MIL, Margaret, about Margaret coming into town for a visit. Initially, Donna is OK with Margaret coming. But the more Margaret talks about her visit, the more Donna feels as though Margaret is making all the decisions and not letting Donna have a say as to when this visit will occur. When Margaret does hear what Donna is saying, it seems as though Margaret merely dismisses Donna's comments. Frustrated, Donna feels that no matter what she says, Margaret just doesn't listen to her. As Donna listens to Margaret talk, Donna thinks to herself, *If she would just stop trying to take over and run the whole show here, I'd say something to her.* But in reality, Donna doesn't know how to say something to Margaret.

> Donna's frustration builds to the point that she feels as though she's going to explode. She knows she needs to get this off her chest, so she decides to talk with her husband, Michael. She tries, but the anger and frustration has built up so much that all she can really do is just spew. And the more she spews, the louder she becomes and the more force her words have. Michael doesn't really say anything – at least anything that feels helpful. And so Donna keeps talking and talking, hoping he'll eventually get it. The more Michael doesn't seem to understand, the more frustrated Donna becomes. Finally, she walks off in a huff and says to herself, *Why doesn't he ever see my side?*

So here you have Mothering Margaret, who is desperately afraid of losing the bond she once had with her son and who tends to blame her DIL for her son distancing himself (both fear and anger at work). And you also have In-the-Middle Michael, who tries to make peace on both sides by explaining each woman's behavior to the other, angering both women in his life (adding frustration and uncertainty). And then you have Doubting Donna, who is so hypersensitive to others' comments that she not only becomes defensive but also feels uncomfortable saying and doing anything for fear she will be judged (adding anxiety and anger). Yikes! No wonder everyone in this pattern is walking on eggshells!

Does She Seem Nuts To You?

As far as patterns go, I would say Does She Seem Nuts to You? is the most challenging pattern of them all because it involves the most extreme behavior. When you have one person who throws a wrench into everyone else's experiences and affects all the relationships around her ... it's agonizing, to say the least.

This is the only pattern that has not one but two possible sets of characters. One set includes the most extreme DIL (Weird Wendy) paired with the most together MIL (Comfortable Carla) and Struggling Steven. The other set includes the most extreme MIL (Off-the-Wall Wanda) paired with the most together DIL (Confident Connie) and Self-Assured Andy. Let's look at the extreme DIL case first.

The most together MIL with the most challenging DIL

Comfortable Carla, who is at ease in most situations, often feels at a loss about how to deal with her DIL, Weird Wendy. Carla is confident and happy about where she is in her life now. She's made it a point to move on, letting her son be the man he now is. She has carved out a new identity that feels good with where she is at this particular stage in her life. And although she tries to connect with Weird Wendy, she continues to find these encounters upsetting, painful and dumbfounding. For example:

Carla wanted to stop by her son and DIL's house to drop off a few baby things she had picked up for them. She called Wendy before heading out just to make sure it was OK to drop in for a minute. Although Wendy was abrupt on the phone, she did say it was OK to come over. Carla was used to this behavior in her DIL, so she didn't really think much about it. Carla arrived, knocked on the door and waited. She waited for what seemed like forever until Wendy finally opened the door just a crack and said, "You can't come in. The baby's asleep." Carla didn't know how to respond. Then Wendy closed the door, leaving Carla on the porch holding a handful of baby clothes!

Struggling Steven is living up to his name. For the most part, he can see what the problem is, but he doesn't know what to do to make things better between not just his wife and mother, but also between his wife and the rest of his family. He loves his wife and wants to make her happy. He's just not sure how to do that, particularly when it comes to their being around everyone else. He doesn't perceive his family the same way she does. Steven often avoids the issues entirely by limiting the couple's time around his mother and/or the rest of the family. Or he makes excuses to them about his wife's behavior. Here's an example:

Steven's family is getting together in the afternoon for Father's Day. Wendy has made it clear that she finds his family – particularly his mother – to be judgmental of her, and she doesn't want to spend the entire afternoon with them. Steven hears what Wendy is saying, but he doesn't see that his family treats her any differently than any other in-law. However, he doesn't want to make things worse, so he just listens to her. After some time, he calls his mother and lets her know that Wendy isn't feeling well, so he and the kids will come over without her around 3 p.m.

Weird Wendy has her own way of viewing the world (and her MIL). Her ability to twist and distort the most innocent verbal exchange or behavior can create a dilemma for anyone on the other side. She really does believe her perspective is right and that anyone disagreeing with her will pay a price. When Wendy feels wronged by someone, she often holds a grudge, refuses to talk with that person and/or makes it difficult for that person to get back into Wendy's good graces. As a result, being around her creates such tension, anxiety and anguish that most people say nothing to her – and so Wendy's odd behaviors go unchallenged. But to Wendy, this just reinforces that she is indeed right. Let me give you an example:

> Wendy's MIL, Carla, is coming over to visit. The last time she was at the house, Carla spent time with her youngest grandson, who then promptly came down with the flu. He had gotten really sick, and the symptoms lasted longer than anyone expected. Wendy believed that Carla was a carrier for the virus because she was the last one to be around her son before he became ill. Even though Carla is completely healthy now and has been for more than a month, Wendy doesn't want to take any more chances. When Carla arrives, Wendy makes it clear to her that she can see and talk to the grandchildren, but she is not allowed to hold or touch them. Stunned, Carla says nothing and complies.

The most together DIL with the most challenging MIL

Now we'll turn to a completely different set of characters, who act out the same pattern with a slightly different flavor. We'll first consider the DIL, Confident Connie, who has really embraced her life as a wife and new mother. She feels comfortable about who she is and where she's going. She knows that she and her husband are on the same page with the important things in life, and that's what she loves about their relationship. Only one person seems to create issues for Confident Connie – her MIL, Off-the-Wall Wanda. No matter what Connie says or does, Wanda ignores her wishes and says and does whatever she wants. Connie finds it difficult to even *want* to spend time with Wanda because the woman always makes every situation about herself. Here's an example:

> As the phone rings, Connie considers whether to answer it. She knows it's her MIL, Wanda, and that answering the phone will mean enduring a 45-minute (minimum) monologue – or quite possibly a rant. Whenever Wanda calls, the older woman monopolizes the whole conversation. It's not that Wanda doesn't

ask about the grandchildren or her son, because she sometimes does ask. However, she never really waits to hear an answer; she's just off onto the next subject or her next opinion. Often, Connie finds herself doing other things while Wanda is talking, interjecting the occasional verbal acknowledgment whenever she can fit it into the conversation. Connie feels frustrated and annoyed, but she doesn't really know what to do. She's tried talking to Wanda, but Wanda doesn't change. And so every time the phone rings, Connie finds herself looking at the caller ID to see if it's Wanda before determining if she's willing to pick up the phone.

Self-Assured Andy knows exactly what his wife is going through with his mother. After all, he grew up with Wanda. In spite of (or maybe because of) his mother's bizarre behavior, Andy has grown into a man who is confident, independent and strong in his beliefs. He puts his mother's behavior into the proper perspective and has learned over the years to take nothing she says or does personally. His relationship with her is limited because he chooses to separate himself from his mother's craziness. For example:

Andy is listening to his wife talk about an incident that occurred with his mother. He understands how his wife feels – he really does. He even empathizes with her frustration. However, he doesn't understand why his wife lets his mother affect her the way she does. It's not as if this is new behavior. His mother has always been like this. Andy listens and eventually either reminds his wife who she's dealing with or lets her know he feels her pain.

When we examine Off-the-Wall Wanda's role in this pattern, we can see that without full awareness, she is trying to control her DIL and son (as well as everyone else) through her extreme behavior. Whether the behavior is outwardly obvious with rants and comments that cross the line, or whether she executes a subtler yet thoroughly punishing withdrawal, the effect is the same – people dread being around her.

Off-the-Wall Wanda's lack of self-awareness leaves her clueless as to why she has the kind of relationships she has with the different people in her family. Let me give you an example:

Wanda is having the family over for dinner. She has made such a big deal about everyone needing to come that most family members feel pressure to not just show up but to stay for a significant length of time. Such pressure docs not make for a fun family gathering. Wanda's son, Andy, and his wife, Connie, have made it clear to Wanda that they cannot stay long because they have another commitment later that evening. When Andy first brought up the prior commitment, Wanda barraged him with questions and accusatory statements. She repeated this performance a few days later and then did it again the day of the family dinner. But Andy and Connie have remained firm on their plans. When they arrive at Wanda's house, Wanda ignores them and barely even says hello. She continues this behavior throughout the dinner, up until Andy and Connie leave. Wanda refuses to forgive them for what she feels is an insult. Wanda believes that Andy and Connie see her as unimportant.

In both of these types of scenarios – whether you're the MIL who's dealing with a Weird Wendy or you're the DIL who's dealing with an Off-the-Wall Wanda – you find it a struggle just to be around your in-law. The difficulty in the relationship often feels insurmountable. In fact, this is the only relationship in your life that gives you this much trouble.

It Is ... What It Is

What makes the It Is ... What It Is pattern so different from the other patterns is that not everyone is having an issue with this relationship. For the most part, the DIL, Transitioned Tracy, is perfectly fine having her relationship with her MIL be whatever it is, without really making it into anything more. However, the MIL, Uncertain Sara, really wants the two of them to have a stronger connection. These two women have different ideas about what they want out of their relationship, and this creates the problem. The other aspect that makes this particular pattern so different is that the husband/son has little or no bearing on how the relationship plays out between his wife and mother, so he is just as likely to be Self-Assured Andy as In-the-Middle Michael or Struggling Steven. This pattern is really just about the two women.

As we examine this pattern, let's check in with Uncertain Sara first. Sara basically has a good heart and is happy that her DIL, Transitioned Tracy, is now in the family. She would just like the relationship to be more than what it is, because she and Tracy act more like acquaintances than family. Uncertain Sara tries different things to engage Tracy, but nothing changes. Sometimes Sara gets a little too close for Tracy's comfort level, and other times she comes across as too distant. Sara is really at a loss about getting closer to Tracy. Here's an example:

> Tracy is getting ready for her little girl's third birthday. She's planning two parties – one with family and one with her daughter's close friends from preschool. Her MIL, Sara, is eager to help. Sara had no daughters of her own, so having a "little girl" party sounds exciting. Sara calls Tracy to see what she might be able to do to help her. Tracy doesn't call her back right away. Sara's not sure what to do now. She calls a couple more times. Then she waits. About a week before the two parties, she calls and Tracy picks up the phone. Sara doesn't know if she should bring up the parties or just let things go. Tracy is pleasant but appears somewhat disengaged with the conversation. Sara is beside herself because she wants to talk with Tracy about how she can help with the parties, but she feels Tracy doesn't want Sara's help. So Sara says nothing about the parties. She hangs up feeling hurt, sad and completely at a loss.

Now let's look at this pattern from Transitioned Tracy's point of view. Tracy feels no need to add Uncertain Sara to her repertoire of friends. She doesn't dislike her MIL; she speaks to her and is certainly pleasant with her, but she is fine with the relationship operating mainly through her husband. Because of Sara's behavior and reactions, Tracy often finds interacting with her tiring because Tracy has to "gear up" whenever she and Sara are together. For example:

> Tracy is at her MIL's house for a few hours before she and her husband leave to go to the airport. Tracy's husband is in the other room talking with his father while Tracy and Sara are in the kitchen. Sara knows Tracy enjoys things like cooking and entertaining. And so Sara talks about recipes she'd like to share with Tracy, what Sara has cooked that was a hit with friends, how Sara used to entertain many years ago and on and on. Tracy is only half listening. It's not that she wants to be rude because she doesn't; it's just that she's heard most all of this before. She finds herself looking at the clock, waiting for the minutes to pass so she and her husband can leave.

In this pattern, it doesn't matter which type of husband or son comes into play because the husband/son does not really affect how the MIL and DIL interact with one another. Whether you have Self-Assured Andy, In-the-Middle Michael or Struggling Steven, the MIL-DIL relationship is not really impacted. However, the relationship between the DIL and her husband *is* impacted.

If Transitioned Tracy is married to Self-Assured Andy, for example, he knows his mother is basically a nice woman but not always easy to be around, so Andy and his wife are on the same page. This allows them to go into situations with his mother from pretty much the same perspective.

However, if Tracy is married to In-the-Middle Michael, he may push her to have a relationship with his mother. He doesn't see how his mother's behavior can be occasionally inconsistent or a bit much at times. This causes fights between Michael and his wife, weakening their marriage.

Struggling Steven's inconsistencies when it comes to the relationship between his mother and his wife also can create problems in his marriage. At times, he understands Tracy's lack of desire to cultivate a relationship with his mother, but other times he struggles with wanting *everyone* to be happy when he sees that his mother is clearly *not* happy.

Struggling Steven's vacillating often creates tension in his marriage and leads to arguments between him and his wife.

As you can see, in all of these patterns (except for Camelot), many of these MILs, DILs and husbands/sons are twisting how they view the others based on their own perceptions. They're then reacting to their perceptions as if those perceptions are The Truth. This often creates a chain reaction that just makes the situation, and ultimately their relationship, get worse.

Although all this may sound like a catch-22, don't get too discouraged. Keep reading, because we're about to move into how to make this relationship better – for everyone involved.

Chapter 7

Perception and Reaction

This chapter deals with the next two elements – one of which you can control and one you can't – that you'll need in order to get a handle on how to create positive change. What you *can't* control is how your MIL or DIL is interpreting what you say and do (in other words, your in-law's perception of your words and actions – regardless of your good intentions). Even so, you certainly can *influence* those perceptions, and shifting your perspective to understand this also helps you to make adjustments in the element that you *can* control – how you react to your in-law's perceptions.

This chapter also offers you some exercises (some for MILs and some for DILs) that will help this information really sink in so you can begin to use it to make things better between you and your in-law. So hang on – relief is in sight!

Perception

Perception is a funny thing. Our different histories and life experiences color and shape how each of us perceives others and their actions. In turn, these things can affect how we feel about ourselves as well. So when someone acts a certain way toward you, how you feel as a result can be different depending on your *perception*. For example, you may feel happy, confused, hurt, unsure or powerless – all depending on how you perceive the other person and what he or she said and did, which is, in turn, influenced by your own history and life experiences.

How many times have you said to someone else or thought to yourself, "My mother-in-law [or daughter-in-law] is so selfish," or maybe you said she was controlling, or even mean, strange or distant. It's much easier to focus on the other person, whether it's your MIL or DIL, because that's what seems to be the source of your hurt or pain. And yet, staying focused on your MIL or DIL doesn't get you any closer to feeling better – in fact, it does just the opposite. You end up feeling powerless.

My own story (remember the Thanksgiving From Hell in Chapter 1?) is a good example. When my DIL and I weren't getting along, I would talk, cry and even sob to my husband about how she always seemed determined to control my time with our granddaughters. I complained that I never seemed to get to spend the one-on-one time with them that I wanted. Not only that, but my DIL made the time I spent with their whole family uncomfortable and tense because I didn't know what to expect from her. Somehow, someway, I'd end up doing something that would make her angry, and then the visit would be ruined. I would always feel frustrated, hurt and even angry at my DIL for how I felt she was treating me.

My whole focus was on what my DIL did or didn't do that made me feel hurt, sad or angry. I really felt helpless to change things. *And I'm a psychotherapist, for goodness sake,* I'd think. *I should know what to do, right?* And yet, I was so focused on how hurt or upset I was that I never thought about how my DIL might be perceiving *my* behavior and how that perception might be contributing to what was going on. I knew the intent behind my behavior was good; I was just trying to be helpful. But that's not necessarily how my DIL perceived it. And once I understood that, I was able to make changes in *my* behavior that helped change how I felt about her and about myself, and that changed our relationship for the better.

As you can see from this example, my initial focus on my DIL's behavior not only did not help, but it made the situation worse because I was anticipating the negative and then got exactly that. So in order

to look at how your behavior may be adding to what's going on between you and your in-law, start by focusing on knocking down the blocks that make it hard to see beyond the hurt, frustration, confusion and anger.

The following exercise in perception will help you begin to knock down these blocks. I will present two separate exercises here – one for MILs and one for DILs – so that you will be able to maintain your focus on your specific in-law. For each exercise, I will first give you the questions, and then I will give you an example of how a DIL or MIL might answer them so you will have a clear understanding of what I'm asking you to do. Then it will be your turn to answer the questions for yourself so you can begin to knock down your own blocks. Go ahead and grab a piece of paper and a pencil or pen, and let's get started!

Perception Exercise for MILs

Think about a situation with your DIL when she was not happy with something you said or did. Consider how you would answer the following questions (but remember to read through my examples below before you actually write out your answers):

1. What behavior did you display or what did you say that upset your DIL?

2. When you did or said this thing, how did your DIL react or respond to you? For example: Did she avoid you for a time, have your son say something to you, say something to you directly or put a wall up between you?

3. Considering the different types of DILs (see Chapter 4 if you need a refresher), think for a moment how someone who is like a Doubting Donna would interpret or perceive your behavior. Then think about how a Weird Wendy and then how a Transitioned Tracy would interpret that same behavior. Now, thinking about which character your DIL is like most of the time, how would

someone who is *that type* perceive the *behavior* you displayed or the words you said?

4. How would this same specific DIL character perceive not just your behavior, but *you* as a person as a result of your behavior?

5. When you said or did whatever it was, what was your intention at the time?

6. How could you do or say things differently to help your DIL perceive you more accurately?

Now take a look at the following example before you begin to answer the questions for yourself, so you can see the types of answers that will be the most useful to you:

1. What behavior did you display or what did you say that upset your DIL?

   I was watching the grandkids, and I cleaned up the kitchen and straightened the house.

2. When you did or said this thing, how did your DIL react or respond to you?

   She didn't say anything, but she was quiet and kind of avoided me – but not so much that it was obvious. If I had said anything about her avoiding me, she would have easily denied it.

3. Considering the different types of DILs (see Chapter 4 if you need a refresher), think for a moment how someone who is like a Doubting Donna would interpret or perceive your behavior. Then think about how a Weird Wendy and then how a Transitioned Tracy would interpret that same behavior. Now, thinking about which character your DIL is like most of the time, how would someone who is *that type* perceive the *behavior* you displayed or the words you said?

   She's a Doubting Donna, so she would have seen me as being intrusive, critical of her housekeeping and probably judgmental.

4. How would this same specific DIL character perceive not just your behavior, but *you* as a person as a result of your behavior?
   She would have seen me as intrusive and as a person who was overly involved with their family.

5. When you said or did whatever it was, what was your intention at the time?
   I just wanted to be helpful. I just wanted to make things easier for her because she was working all day.

6. How could you do or say things differently to help your DIL perceive you more accurately?
   I could have let her know that I wanted to do something to help her out and to make things easier for her. I could have asked her if she would mind me helping out before just jumping in to do it.

OK, MILs, now it's *your* turn to answer these questions and to take a look at how your DIL might perceive your actions. By the way, don't worry if you find you're struggling a bit with this exercise. It does take time to think through these questions. But trust me, the effort will be well worth it.

DILs, below are the questions for *you*. Just as I did for the MILs, I'll give you the questions first and then an example of how you might answer them to make it clear what I'm asking. After you've read through the questions and the example, it will be *your* turn to answer the questions.

Perception Exercise for DILs

Think about a situation with your MIL when she was not happy with something you said or did. Consider how you would answer the following questions (but remember to read through my examples below before you actually write out your answers):

1. What behavior did you display or what did you say that upset your MIL?

2. When you did or said this thing, how did your MIL react or respond to you? For example: Did she say something directly to you, avoid you, say something to your husband about your actions or visibly tense up around you?

3. Considering the different types of MILs (see Chapter 3 if you need a refresher), think for a moment how someone who is like a Mothering Margaret would interpret or perceive your behavior. Then think about how an Off-the-Wall Wanda and then how an Uncertain Sara would interpret that same behavior. Now, thinking about which character your MIL is like most of the time, how would someone who is *that type* perceive the *behavior* you displayed or the words you said?

4. How would this same specific MIL character perceive not just your behavior, but *you* as a person as a result of your behavior?

5. When you said or did whatever it was, what was your intention at the time?

6. How could you do or say things differently to help your MIL perceive you more accurately?

Now, read the following example before writing down your own answers so you can get a better sense of the types of responses that will help you the most:

1. What behavior did you display or what did you say that upset your MIL?

   I didn't say anything directly to her, but I know my feelings showed in my behavior. I kept my distance from her, and I gave short responses when she tried to talk to me.

2. When you did or said this thing, how did your MIL react or respond to you?

   At first she kept trying harder to talk to me, but then she eventually stayed away from me.

3. Considering the different types of MILs (see Chapter 3 if you need a refresher), think for a moment how someone who is like a Mothering Margaret would interpret or perceive your behavior. Then think about how an Off-the-Wall Wanda and then how an Uncertain Sara would interpret that same behavior. Now, thinking about which character your MIL is like most of the time, how would someone who is *that type* perceive the *behavior* you displayed or the words you said?

   I think she's an Uncertain Sara, and so she would have
   perceived my behavior as rude and inconsiderate.

4. How would this same specific MIL character perceive not just your behavior, but *you* as a person as a result of your behavior?

   She would have seen me as childish.

5. When you said or did whatever it was, what was your intention at the time?

   I kind of wanted her to know I was upset without having
   to get into anything with her.

6. How could you do or say things differently to help your MIL perceive you more accurately?

   Well, I think she got the message that I was upset,
   but I wouldn't want her to think I'm childish. I could
   have been more clear about what I wanted or needed
   beforehand, and that would have eliminated the
   problem altogether.

As you can probably see, for both MILs and DILs, this exercise is about making sure your actions really reflect your true intention – and it's as useful for MILs as it is for DILs. What typically happens for all of us is that because *we* know what our intentions are, we assume others will know what they are as well. We assume our intent is clear in our actions because it is clear within us. After all, I couldn't for the life of me understand how my DIL saw my actions as intrusive or controlling. I was just trying to be helpful! Couldn't she see that? Well, the truth is that no, she couldn't see that – not unless she somehow could have read my mind! And no one is really good at that.

Reaction

The flip side of perception is reaction. When you perceive a person's behavior, you react to it. This in turn will cause the other person to react to *you*, then you react to *her*, and on and on it goes. So of course when you react to your MIL or DIL and she reacts back, a snowball effect can easily ensue. And it's this snowball effect that can create such damage in your relationship because things can *really* get out of hand.

To avoid this, use the following exercise to help you recognize how your reactions can affect your in-law's reaction to you. Again, I will present two separate exercises – one for MILs and one for DILs – so that you will be able to maintain your focus on your specific in-law. After each set of questions, I will again give an example of the types of answers that would be most useful so you can get a clearer understanding of how this exercise works. Still have your piece of paper and pencil or pen handy? Good. Dive in!

Reaction Exercise for MILs

Think about an interaction you had with your DIL where your feelings were stirred up. Then write down your answers to the following questions:

1. What feeling was stirred up inside you?

2. When you felt this way, how did this feeling show in your behavior?
   Now, some of you may think you can hide your feelings pretty well. But believe me, feelings have a way of showing in our behaviors even when we don't realize it. For example, did you feel yourself getting edgy around her, putting up walls, talking less when you're with her or pulling back?

3. If someone else – a friend or an acquaintance – behaved the same way toward you that you behaved toward your DIL, how would you feel?

4. How would you then react to that person?

5. How did your DIL react or respond to your behavior?

6. How could your behavior be directly related to your DIL's reaction?

OK, now that you've read the questions, let me give you an example of how you might answer them, and then you can go back through the questions and answer them for yourself.

1. What feeling was stirred up inside you?
   I was hurt, embarrassed and frustrated.

2. When you felt this way, how did this feeling show in your behavior?
   I made a snide comment, and then I stopped talking altogether.

3. If someone else – a friend or an acquaintance – behaved the same way toward you that you behaved toward your DIL, how would you feel?
   I would have been taken aback. I'd feel so uncomfortable that I'd want to get away from the person.

4. How would you then react to that person?
   I would have stopped talking to the person and would have made an excuse to get away.

5. How did your DIL react or respond to your behavior?
   She started to say something back to me and then stopped; she then said she forgot she had an appointment, and she left.

6. How could your behavior be directly related to your DIL's reaction?
   I think I made her feel so uncomfortable that she just needed to get away from me.

Reaction Exercise for DILs

Think about an interaction you had with your MIL where your feelings were stirred up. Then write down your answers to the following questions:

1. What feeling was stirred up inside you?

2. When you felt this way, how did this feeling show in your behavior? Now, some of you may think you can hide your feelings pretty well. But believe me, feelings have a way of showing in our behaviors even when we don't realize it. For example, did you feel yourself erecting a wall between you, getting edgy around her, disengaging or pulling back from her, or talking less when you're together?

3. If someone else – a friend or an acquaintance – behaved the same way toward you that you behaved toward your MIL, how would you feel?

4. How would you then react to that person?

5. How did your MIL react or respond to your behavior?

6. How could your behavior be directly related to your MIL's reaction?

OK, DILs, here is an example of how you might answer these questions. Once you've read through this example, go back to the questions above and complete them for yourself. You'll start to realize some pretty amazing things about yourself *and* your MIL!

1. What feeling was stirred up inside you?
   I was angry.

2. When you felt this way, how did this feeling show in your behavior?
   I shut down. I avoided my MIL. I let my husband talk to her whenever she called. And whenever she tried to talk to me, I just ignored her request.

3. If someone else – a friend or an acquaintance – behaved the same way toward you that you behaved toward your MIL, how would you feel?

I would feel hurt and probably confused because I wouldn't understand why the other person was doing that.

4. How would you then react to that person?

I would probably just stay away from the person because it would be too uncomfortable to try to find out what happened. But not knowing what was wrong would make my stomach churn.

5. How did your MIL react or respond to your behavior?

She kept trying to talk to me. She talked to my husband about why I wasn't talking to her.

6. How could your behavior be directly related to your MIL's reaction?

I think I caused her to act like that because I never gave her a reason.

After having completed this exercise, you probably have a better understanding of your actions and reactions and how they affect your MIL's or DIL's actions and reactions to *you*. But before you start applying this to your own life, let me share one more very important point to remember in all of this: *Do not focus on whether your behavior or your in-law's behavior is good or bad, right or wrong.* None of that really matters because it's not about good or bad, right or wrong. It's about your perceptions and your reactions. It's about being clear on what it is you want to convey with your words and behaviors. Keep your eyes on the prize: making conscious choices about what you say and what you do so that your words and actions best reflect your true intention.

Chapter 8

When Your DIL Is a Doubting Donna

If your DIL is a Doubting Donna, this chapter is for you (no matter what type of MIL you are). So if your DIL's typical behavior includes defensiveness, being hot and cold toward you (one day she's fine with you, and the next day she's upset with you), wanting or needing to be in control (especially when the situation has to do with you) and hyper-sensitivity toward anything a person may say or do that may be different from what she believes, the strategies outlined here should help. Part of the challenge with a Doubting Donna is that not only has she not resolved the issues she has with her own mother, but also she may be completely unaware that she even has such issues to resolve. So what can MILs do with DILs like this? Plenty!

Tool 1: Check Your Mothering at the Door

Chances are, you probably don't even realize you're doing anything "Mom-like" because this is just what you've been doing for years, your intention is honorable, or sometimes the way you say things or how you present yourself gives off an authoritative air. This "authoritative air" could be in your confident tone of voice, in your body language or even just in the fact that you speak up at all. It may also be that you're just trying to be helpful or your tendency is to be opinionated or to take charge of situations. Regardless, to a Doubting Donna, this behavior oozes "Mom," and because of her issues with her own mother, this isn't going to work for her. So here are some pointers on how you can best use this tool:

- **Pay attention to how your words and behaviors come across** (for a refresher, see the perception section of Chapter 7). Remember that the issue here is really about *how your DIL may interpret your actions*, not how anyone else would interpret them, and not even what you meant to convey.

- Before you say or do anything, **ask yourself what your intentions really are and how you can adjust your words and actions so that you will come across less like a mom.**

- **State your intentions and ask for your DIL's thoughts about what it is you want to do.** This will make your DIL less likely to go into her hypersensitive mode and less likely to misperceive your actions.

Before I show you an example of why these strategies work, let's first have a look at this familiar scenario:

Your DIL and son have invited you over for dinner. When you arrive, you see your DIL in the kitchen working away, preparing dinner. You want to help, so you casually comment, "Let me help you with dinner," and then you jump right in. Your DIL doesn't say anything negative about your helping, but you notice she is not really saying much of anything at all – and you start to feel a bit of an unseasonable chill in the air.

Now let's look at how this scene might play out differently if you instead use the strategies outlined above:

Your DIL and son have invited you over for dinner. When you arrive, you see your DIL in the kitchen working away, preparing dinner. You want to help, so you casually say to your DIL, "I would love to help you with dinner. It would give us a chance to catch up. Would you like some help?"

Can you feel the difference? In the first scenario, you certainly have good intentions, but your DIL has no idea what is behind your action. All she sees is that you suddenly jump in to prepare dinner. And if she's a Doubting Donna, then her lack of self-confidence in who she is, her self-doubt and her hypersensitivity to being seen in a negative way by others will cause her to experience this "jumping in" as an indication that she is not doing something right. She will think that you are criticizing how she's preparing dinner, that you're implying she's a bad cook and you're taking over.

In the second scenario, however, you actually state your intentions and you ask your DIL what she thinks of what it is you want to do. There is less room for your DIL to "fill in the blanks." In other words, when we don't have all the information from someone in a given situation, we naturally fill in the blanks with what we fear the most – we all do this without necessarily being aware that we're doing it. But by stating your intentions out loud, you aren't leaving any blanks for your DIL to fill in. Your words and actions don't set off her alarm bells, so she doesn't feel the need to be defensive.

Now, even in the second scenario, your DIL may say she doesn't want your help. If that happens, please don't take it personally. She may want (or need) to show you *and herself* that she can do it on her own. And that's OK. You can still stand in the kitchen and chat with her while she's cooking dinner. The difference is that she knows your intention and she feels you respect her because you *asked* if you could help; you didn't just decide for yourself. Here's another example:

You just left the store and are heading home. You have some things for your son and DIL in the car, and since you are going right by their house anyway, you decide to stop and drop them off. You knock and go into the house, searching around a bit until you find your DIL coming down the stairs. You let her know you just came by to drop these few things off on your way home from the store. She seems a bit distant, but since she often responds that way, you're not at all surprised.

Now take a look at how this same scenario is likely to unfold if you use these new strategies:

You just left the store and are heading home. You have some things for your son and DIL in the car, and since you are going right by their house anyway, you think about stopping by to drop them off. You call your DIL and say, "Hi, it's me. I'm on my way home, and I have some things for you that I would love to drop off if you're going to be home. Is this a good time, or would you rather I come later today or tomorrow? Either is fine with me." Your DIL lets you know that it's a little hectic at their house right now, but if you don't mind the chaos, stopping by now would be just fine.

Again, can you feel how different the second scenario is from the first? It just feels more complete, more thoughtful. The helpful intention is the same, and much of the behavior is the same. The main difference is that you're stating your intention *before* you act, you're asking for your DIL's thoughts about what you want to do, and you are also giving her some choice in the matter. Even if that doesn't seem like such a big deal *to you*, if your DIL is a Doubting Donna, it will make a difference like night and day *to her*.

But what if you *do* state your intentions, and yet your DIL still misperceives them because she hears only *part* of what you say? Believe me, this can also happen, depending on your DIL. You can use certain strategies to protect yourself from being judged in this way (even though you're doing all the right things). But first, let me explain what is happening with your DIL.

As with many Doubting Donnas, your DIL may be a people pleaser. If so, she will be so uncomfortable with the idea that anyone might be mad at her for something she's said or done that she is likely to agree with others (including you) or to say that something is OK even if it isn't what she wants. As time goes on, she will eventually realize that she's not happy with what she agreed to, so she may try to undo it. Then she will become so anxious with the idea that she will be judged by others for this that she will end up judging *them* and blaming *them* for twisting things around or for pushing her into something. As you can imagine, this can really turn into quite a mess, mainly because your DIL cannot own up to what *she* created. This then puts you in a position where you feel uneasy around her, start watching what you say and ultimately lose trust in her. This may sound like an impossible situation, but fear not. There *is* a way out.

Let me start by saying you do *not* want to say anything directly to your Doubting Donna about this because she will never be able to admit what she did (especially because she may not even be consciously aware that she did it). The best thing to do, at least initially, is to protect yourself. If she hints or directly asks for your thoughts about something, skirt around the issue with her. Let her make the decision without any suggestions from you.

I know this is not a natural reaction. With most people, you can make a suggestion or think out loud with them, and then they will make their decision and be fine with it. But in this case, you are not dealing with most people. Remember, in this case, your DIL will hear a suggestion and then believe she needs to take that suggestion and act on it so that you won't get mad at her – even though that is the furthest thing from your mind. *To you it's about making suggestions, but to Doubting Donna, it's about pleasing you.* Let me give you an example:

Your son and your DIL, Donna, invite you for dinner. When you get there, Donna begins talking about wanting to paint her living room and get some new throw pillows for her couch. You immediately start to say something about the new colors that are popular right now, but then you catch yourself. You've been here before with her and you don't want to cause another uncomfortable situation. So you sit back and listen to what she's saying. You ask her some questions about what colors she likes, what her vision is for the room, and on and on. And you're extremely careful not to suggest *anything*. You continue asking her questions, helping her get clear on what her vision is and allowing her to make her own decisions.

In this example, not only have you made it a point to not recreate an ugly situation, but you've also helped your DIL sort through her own feelings so she can learn to trust herself and her decisions. You could not have given her a better gift!

Tool 2: Treat Your DIL as an Adult

You may think that you already *do* treat your Doubting Donna DIL like an adult, and if so, that this next strategy doesn't really apply to you. But don't be so quick to skip over this one. What I mean is that it's important to treat your DIL more as an *equal* and less as a *daughter-like figure*. Yes, she's younger than you. Yes, she has less life experience than you. And yes, she doesn't have the knowledge base you've developed over the years that has given you the wisdom you have today. However, this doesn't negate the fact that she *does* have life experiences. She may not have *as many* of them as you do, but she does have some just the same. So what are a few simple ways to show your DIL that you see her as an adult?

Get to know your DIL for who she is – find out what makes her, well, her. It's one thing to know your DIL as your son's wife, but it's another to know her for who she is as a unique individual. What is her personal style? What kinds of things does she like, and what does she dislike? What are her favorite foods? What does she do in her free time? Is she a "glass half empty" or a "glass half full" kind of person? Is she a social butterfly or does she stay more to herself? Explore the answers to many of these types of questions until you feel you really know who your DIL is.

Another way to get to know your DIL is to look at who she is in relation to you – seeing both how she is similar to you and how she's different from you. By doing this, you can see her more objectively, and you'll be less likely to take her words or actions personally. The more you see her as an individual, the better equipped you are to put your interactions with her in perspective. Here's an example:

> You are helping your DIL get the kids ready to go to the pool. As you help the youngest one get her swimsuit on, your DIL makes a cutting remark to you about how you're going about the job. ("Hey, Grandma, don't you know how to put a swimsuit on?") It isn't just her words that make the comment sound so harsh – it's her biting tone.

Now granted, no matter how well you understand your DIL, her words may sound callous. But really having a sense of who your DIL is can help you put those words in perspective. And by doing so, you are less likely to be caught off guard by her remarks, and you're in a better place to know how to respond. Remember, too, that Doubting Donnas aren't really trying to push their MILs away completely. Deep down, this DIL wants to have some kind of relationship with you. But because of her unresolved issues with her own mother, she struggles with where you fit into her world.

So what *could* you say to a cutting remark like that? Make it simple. Say something that leaves the door open instead of something that slams it shut. You could say, "Ouch, that cut deep," or "Wow, what was *that* about?" or even, "*What* did you say?" (all in a fairly lighthearted tone). The goal is to say something that lets your DIL know you are responding to her brashness, but at the same time, you aren't trying to get into a discussion about it. You want to make your point, but you want to leave it with her to ponder, not counter with a harsh comment of your own. More times than not, you will notice your DIL start to backpedal and eventually stop this kind of behavior.

Find something your DIL does well and let her teach you. This is really very simple. Your DIL is bound to be good at something or know some things you don't know. Ask her how she does this thing she does well or ask her to tell you about this bit of knowledge she has that you don't. This not only lets your Doubting Donna know that you see her as an adult with knowledge and experience that you don't have, but it also lets her see that you value her.

For example, when my son and DIL were first married, my DIL worked in the insurance business. She dealt with all different kinds of insurance and knew more than I ever could on the subject. So whenever my husband or I had general questions about insurance, policies, claims or whatever, we called our DIL. This was her area of expertise, not ours, and we respected her knowledge in this area. Not only was what she had to say helpful to us, but it also let her see that we valued her knowledge and expertise. *And we really did.* We could have called our own insurance agent with our questions, but we really wanted to call our DIL.

Another way to think of your DIL as an adult and treat her as such is by thinking about your different close friends. Most likely, you have many friends of different ages – some are older and some are younger – and yet you learn from each of them, just as each of them learns from you. Your DIL is no different. In many ways, she is like a new friend – and as I explained in Chapter 2, friendships take time. When you're developing a new friendship, it's important that you tread lightly and show yourself slowly. You naturally take care to be thoughtful of the other person's perspectives and respectful of your differences, don't you? Well, why would you do anything less with your DIL?

Even if your DIL has been around for a while and can't really be considered a *new* friend, you can still use these tools. The truth is that it's *never* too late to start.

Chapter 9

When Your DIL Is a Weird Wendy

This chapter is for all MILs who have a Weird Wendy for a DIL. As you may recall, Wendy is often distant, aloof and unwilling to engage with anyone, particularly her MIL. When she does interact with someone – whether it's a friend, her own family or her husband's family – she typically perceives the person through a distorted filter. This creates confusion, tension and misunderstandings because to Wendy, *her perspective is the only correct perspective.* She's convinced that everyone else does things to hurt her, upset her, challenge her and embarrass her, and on and on it goes.

Is there any hope for making things better when you're dealing with such an extreme personality type? Weird Wendy is definitely the most challenging of all the DILs to deal with. But have faith. You *can* improve your relationship – trust me.

To be successful in this, you must plan ahead of time how you want to handle situations that may arise. You also must make sure that the way you behave or what you say is as clear as possible. The tools in this section will help you do just that. But throughout this entire process, you must keep three vital points in mind. First, *never take what Wendy says or does personally.* I know that's hard to do, particularly when Wendy pushes all your buttons. But if you focus on the fact that she isn't singling you out – she treats all people this same way – this gets easier to see.

Second, *shift your expectations*. With a Weird Wendy, you will never have a close, warm relationship. But what you *can* have is a change in Wendy's behavior that makes the relationship easier. It isn't about building an emotional connection with her; it's about getting her to change her behavior.

And third, *don't expect big changes overnight*. Remember that major modifications in behavior take time and usually occur in baby steps. So after the first few times you use these tools, you may see only a small change – and it's very possible that you won't see any change at all! Don't get discouraged. As you keep at it, consistently using the tools presented here time and time again, you will indeed see that *shift happens!*

Tool 1: Perfect the Double Bind

One thing about Weird Wendy that can work to your advantage is that she's often predictable in her over-the-top behavior. For example, you may *know* that whenever she's upset with you she makes it a point to avoid you in very obvious ways. Or she may tend to isolate herself at family gatherings by spending her time in a room away from everyone else. The genius of the Double Bind is that it uses Wendy's predictability to shake things up a bit. It gets your DIL off her game, so to speak, so that she will be more apt to play nice.

Here's how the Double Bind works: When you want Wendy to do something different from her usual, predictable behavior, **state out loud what you anticipate she will do or say before she has a chance to do or say it**.

So for example, let's say your DIL has a tendency to withdraw or pull away when you do or say something she doesn't like. Remember, when she acts like this, it's because in her eyes you are not there for her, and she's reacting to this belief or perception. So to use the Double Bind, you would say something like this to her:

"I know you're going to be upset, and you'll probably want to keep your distance from me, but I'm really sorry I can't watch the grandkids that night. If it were any other night, I'd love to, but I have a commitment that night."

I'm sure some of you are probably thinking, *Is she for real? No one would be that unreasonable or misperceive that situation.* Trust me, with Weird Wendy, it happens – even in the most innocent of situations. Let's take the example mentioned above about Wendy isolating herself at family gatherings. To use the Double Bind, you'd go into the room where she is and say something like this:

"Wendy! I thought I'd find you in here. I know you'd rather stay in here and read, but I could really use your help in the kitchen. Could you please give me a hand?" You then stand there, saying nothing more, and wait for a response – whether that's a verbal response ("Um ... OK ...") or a behavioral one (she actually puts her book down and starts to get up).

It is *extremely important* that when you use the Double Bind that you **make sure you are pleasant and genuine when you are talking with your DIL**. If you have any edge to your voice, or if you sound even slightly sarcastic or display any trace of an attitude, your Weird Wendy will pick that up and she'll react to *that* instead of to your words. This in turn will cause more problems than you had to begin with. So be sure to calm down and come from a safe, neutral place emotionally before you speak to her.

The reason the Double Bind works is that Weird Wendy likes to feel in control of everything – herself, her environment and even you. She craves control because she is sure that everyone else, including you, is trying to manipulate her, pressure her or demand something of her – and even though this isn't really true, you can never use reason and logic to convince her otherwise. That's why she feels so justified in her over-the-top actions.

But by telling her how you expect her to act and displaying that you can predict how she'll behave, you make it difficult for Wendy to then carry out those predicted behaviors. How can she now display the behavior you've told her you *know* she's going to do? Using the Double Bind disarms her and takes her power away because she is no longer in control! And because you are being pleasant and genuine when you use this tool, you won't be causing confrontation or creating any sort of a scene.

But what if she still goes ahead and does the behavior you've just told her that you know she's probably going to do? (Sometimes Weird Wendy can't stop herself.) It's really OK because she *knows* that you knew she'd behave that way because you told her so. This will not sit well with her at all, and she probably will be less likely to display that predicted behavior the next time.

Tool 2: Mirror Your DIL's Words

This tool involves verbalizing Weird Wendy's behavior or words out loud to her – but in a neutral (not mocking or attacking) way. By doing this, you put her in the position of having to not only look at her behavior, but also to be accountable for her actions and her words. Here's an example of how it works:

> Your DIL isn't happy with something you did or said, so she tries to impose rules about how you can spend time with your grand-children. You want to take them out separately to have a special day with each one individually, but your DIL says you can't take one unless you take them all. With a somewhat confused look on your face and using a pleasant and sincere tone, you say, "So you're saying I can't take the grandkids individually so they can have some special one-on-one time with me?" You say nothing more, allowing the silence to just hang in the air.

By repeating your DIL's words, you give her a chance to hear how over-the-top those words sound. You are mirroring them back to her and holding her accountable. If she says, "No, that's not what I'm saying," then ask her to clarify what she said. If her reply is still off-the-wall, then repeat the process once more, saying: "So let me see if I have it this time. You're saying _____." Keep doing this until your DIL's response makes more sense, or until it becomes apparent to everyone present that something is amiss in what she is saying.

If you reach the point where it's apparent to everyone else that your Weird Wendy's behavior is indeed off-the-wall, or if she agrees that the over-the-top statement you mirror back to her is indeed her position, then you pull out some heavier artillery. It's time to combine mirroring with the Double Bind – while adding the little twist of giving her an option. Here's an example of what you would say in using this strategy in the previous scenario:

> "I know it may mean I don't get to see the grandkids at all [*Double Bind*], but you wanting me to take all the kids at the same time [*mirroring*] is not giving them a chance to feel special, and I really think it's important that they get some special time just for themselves. So, what if I have special time with one, and then the next time I do a group thing with all the grandkids, and then I have special time with another, then do the group thing again, and then have special time with the third one?" [*option*]

By giving your DIL options for things that you *can* do that still address her concerns, you come across as reasonable, and you show that you're trying to take her thoughts into consideration. Again, the important thing is to **mirror back first, and if that isn't enough, try mirroring back and adding the Double Bind with an option twist.**

As useful as these tools can be with Weird Wendy, she may be so unpredictable at times that you cannot plan ahead and strategize because she is always catching you off guard (or because her words are so off-the-wall that there is no way to have a comeback). You may also have a Weird Wendy who absolutely refuses to have any contact with you (she ignores your calls and emails and acts as though you don't exist). Each of these extreme situations calls for some special tools.

119

Tool 3: Dealing With Extreme Unpredictability

Are you constantly left with your mouth hanging open whenever you interact with your DIL? Does she always seem to have the upper hand, no matter what? Don't waste any time blaming yourself for not being able to anticipate what she will say or do next. Instead, **think of some generic responses** you can use when she makes *that* statement or does *that* behavior. It can be something as simple as just saying, "Really?" Or, "Did you just say _____?" (while repeating back to her what she just said in that innocent, confused, did-I-hear-you-right tone of voice). This is similar to the mirroring technique in Tool 2, but this time you have no expectations. Also, here you are mirroring back in a lighthearted way, using a tone that reflects a question, not a statement.

Another way to respond is to **just laugh**. Seriously. Laugh out loud, with that oh-you-are-so-funny laugh. I'm not suggesting that you laugh in a mean way that would make fun of your DIL, but in a way that speaks to the craziness of what you just experienced – as if you're both in on some great joke together. Laughter often sends a message that no words ever can.

Tool 4: Dealing With Extreme Cold-Shoulder Treatment

This is one of the toughest spots for any MIL to find herself in. When your DIL won't even talk to you, let alone give the two of you a chance to fix your broken relationship, you can feel utterly powerless. Even so, the multiple steps outlined in this tool will indeed help you melt some of the ice that has built up between the two of you. Before we start, let me emphasize that you will need to exercise patience – and lots of it. And you will also need to put your hurt and angry feelings aside for a bit. Allow me to explain.

If your DIL is not responding to your phone calls and emails, if she's not letting you spend time with your grandkids because of what's going on between the two of you, it is usually because she feels so upset or angry or hurt that she cannot allow herself to be around you. Now remember, this is less about truth and more about perception.

Think about this for a minute – in one corner, you have Weird Wendy, who feels so emotional about something she believes you've said or done that she would rather avoid all contact with you. And then in the other corner, there's you, who feel powerless and victimized by your DIL and her actions. Can you see the impasse? Both you and your DIL feel the same way. You both feel that the other one is causing *all* the pain. And it's these feelings that don't allow either of you to move off your emotional points. So the first step in this tool is to **identify the fact that you're at a true stalemate**, with each of you feeling victimized by the other.

Once you recognize yourself in this description, it is vital that you then **understand that your feelings of victimization are preventing you from hearing *anything* your DIL is saying.** If you're sure this doesn't apply to you, here's a good test: Think about the conversations you've had with others about your DIL. Do you *always* talk about *what she's doing to you?* If so, then you are focused on your own victimization, and you are keeping yourself locked in the stalemate. On top of that, you are indeed giving your DIL all the power in the relationship.

Moving forward will be impossible unless you fully grasp that this is not about who is right and who is wrong. You must keep your focus on your goal – whether that's having a relationship with your DIL, getting to see your grandkids again or whatever it is you want that you don't currently have. Every time you lapse into right-wrong, win-lose thinking, you have to put your focus back on your goal.

Next, write your DIL some letters of appreciation. (This works much better if the message is in letters, not emails.) Now, I know that some of you are thinking, *Is she nuts? Why would I want to write letters of appreciation to a woman who treats me like this? What is there to appreciate?* But you must remember that your DIL is the woman your son chose. He loves her. She makes him happy. And at least in some small way, that should make *you* happy, too (regardless of all the other stuff going on).

So the first letter might be about how much you appreciate your DIL for loving your son. And then maybe write a letter about how much you appreciate her for being the mother of your grandkids. Another letter could be about what positive things your DIL has brought to your family, and so on.

As I warned you earlier, change will not happen overnight, so this is where patience really comes in. Even if you don't get a response, keep the letters going out to her. They don't have to be long – the key is to make sure they say what you want them to say. And these letters *cannot* reflect any of your negative, victim-like feelings at all. That is why I mentioned earlier that you need to put your feelings aside.

Once your DIL starts to acknowledge you a bit, you can begin the next step – **listening to her and acknowledging her experiences**. This is *not* about agreeing with her perceptions, and it's *not* about arguing with what she has to say. Listening and acknowledging is just that – *listening* to your DIL while she expresses her feelings about something you've done or said and then *acknowledging* those feelings by repeating back to her in your own words what you heard her say and the feeling she is expressing. For example:

Your DIL says to you, "You involved all the family with our problems."

Then you say back to her, "So you're saying you are upset with me because I shared with other family members what was going on between us?"

or

Your DIL says to you, "Every time you come over, you make some comment about the way my house looks. And you make this face whenever you watch how I deal with one of the kids."

Then you say back to her, "So you feel like I'm judging you whenever I come over to see you?"

By responding in this way, you are hearing what your DIL has to say, asking her for clarification and acknowledging what she is experiencing. It doesn't mean she's right, it just means this is how she is experiencing you.

But what happens if (or rather *when*) your DIL says, "Yes, that's *exactly* how I feel!" Your tendency may be to get defensive and try to justify what you said or did, but resist that temptation because it will undo *everything* you've accomplished up to that point. Instead, muster up some compassion and **let her know how bad you feel that she took your words or actions in the manner she did**. So for example, you could say, "Oh, wow! I had *no idea* that's how my words/actions made you feel. It was *never* my intent to make you feel that way. I can see why you would be upset if you thought that's what I meant." Or "Oh, I am *so* sorry. I never meant to make you feel bad – really! I would be upset, too, if I thought someone had those intentions." And then either ask your DIL what you can do in the future to help fix this misperception, or let her know you'll pay more attention to what you say and do to prevent it from happening again – which leads us right into the final step, below.

To make sure these misunderstandings don't creep back into your relationship, **make sure that from now on, you state your intentions clearly.** (For a refresher, see the tools for Doubting Donna and the discussion of perception in Chapter 7.) This will help keep your DIL from feeling as though she needs to build the wall back up.

You can use this tool in as many situations as needed to melt the ice. Remember that your DIL wants to be heard, and she wants to feel that you understand how she feels. Once she believes you are really listening to her feelings and acknowledging them, she will be more open to seeing you accurately and allowing the relationship to have more give and take.

Since this is a lot to take in, let me offer a short recap of the steps for this tool:

- Recognize the stalemate.
- Look at how your feelings of being victimized by your DIL are preventing you from hearing anything she is saying.
- Write appreciation letters to your DIL.
- Listen and acknowledge your DIL's feelings and experiences.

- Express true compassion for those feelings and let your DIL know that how she interpreted your words or actions wasn't how you intended them.

- Be clear in verbalizing the intent behind your behavior.

Chapter 10

When Your DIL Is a Transitioned Tracy

Any MIL who has a Transitioned Tracy for a DIL will find the tools in this chapter quite helpful. As you may remember, Transitioned Tracy's relationship with her mother while she was growing up had its ups and downs, but now she has worked through many of those issues. At this point in her life, Tracy is fairly confident and proud of what she's accomplished – and fairly independent, as well.

But as her MIL, you may feel at a loss in knowing how to interact with her because while she is often pleasant and maybe even somewhat friendly when you're together, she doesn't go out of her way to establish a relationship with you that's separate from being your son's wife. There's an air about Transitioned Tracy, a certain invulnerability or aloofness that leaves you feeling a bit uncertain – uncertain about your role with her, about how to talk with her, about how to create a connection with her, and on and on the list goes.

This uncertainty creates a bit of a struggle in this relationship because your DIL picks up on it (partly because she can feel it but also because your behavior seems confusing in so many ways), and then *she* feels uncertain about *you*. The cycle then just keeps perpetuating itself. This may be easier to understand if you take a look at things from the perspective of *your DIL*. So for the example below, we're going to look at a situation from Tracy's point of view. Here goes:

Your father has had major surgery and is convalescing at home. You try to run to your parents' house several times a week to see your dad and to help your mother. On top of this you are also trying to be there for your own husband and kids. You want to continue helping your father, but you are feeling the toll it's taking on you. At one point, you are talking with your MIL, and you mention to her that you need her help on this one particular day. You need her to pick up the kids from aftercare while you take your dad to his post-surgery doctor's appointment and then watch them until you get home.

Your MIL has mentioned to you on several occasions that she's willing to help out whenever you need her to. And although you rarely ask your MIL to do anything for you, this time you really need the help, so you go ahead and ask. But instead of eagerly agreeing to help, she hesitates and even starts to stammer a bit. She's not saying yes or no; she's not really saying anything. Finally, after a fairly long pause, she says, "Well, I guess I can do that." You immediately sense ambivalence. You're not sure what that's all about, but you feel either she doesn't *want* to help or she *can't* really help but doesn't want to say no – or she has some other reason that you can't even imagine. What you *do* know, however, is that she seems hesitant. *I don't have the time or the patience to figure this out,* you think. *I just need some help.* So you decide to ask your girlfriend for help instead.

As you can see, your DIL has *no clue* what you're thinking or what's behind your hesitancy. And although you may have been stammering because you were taken by surprise *and* you were trying to remember your schedule and think through the logistics of doing what your DIL was asking, your DIL doesn't know that. All she can see is your behavior. If your uncertainty shows every once in awhile, that's one thing. However, if it comes out fairly frequently, you'll find developing any kind of real connection with your DIL to be difficult. So what can MILs do when their DILs keep them at arm's length? Read on!

Tool 1: Shift Your Expectations

Your expectations for a warm relationship with your Transitioned Tracy DIL combined with your uncertainty and your not knowing how to act around her create the type of confused loop described above. We all have expectations; it's natural. But sometimes those expectations need to be tweaked a bit. In this case, because your expectations aren't met (your DIL doesn't act in the way you expect or hope she will), you begin second-guessing yourself, hesitating, trying too hard to be close to her or just plain trying too hard in general. All that often makes your behavior look scattered and odd, which understandably frustrates your DIL. But if you can begin to shift your expectations, your uncertainty will start to disappear, and so will a big part of the problem.

The first thing to keep in mind when using this tool is that the relationship you *do* have with your DIL will probably never measure up to your initial high expectations. You will never be best friends or even really close to Transitioned Tracy. So putting your relationship in perspective will go a long way in helping you to relax around your DIL. This is true because right now, your expectations of what you *want* or *hope* the relationship to be are getting in your way of allowing the relationship to just *be what it is*. You feel this stress and emotional turmoil directly, and your DIL feels it indirectly. Now, some of you may be thinking, *I don't really feel things* that *intensely,* or *My expectations aren't* that *crazy.* And you may be right. But the bottom line is that even normal expectations come with emotional attachments that everyone who's around you can feel. Shifting your expectations works because it allows you not only to better align what you want with the reality of your situation, but also to feel better about yourself, your DIL and your relationship with her.

The following questions will take you through some helpful steps for beginning to shift your expectations. Read over the questions and

127

then read through the sample response that follows so that you have a better idea where this exercise is going. Then it's your turn to answer. Get a paper and pencil so you can actually write your answers down; that will make your responses much more precise and it will enable you to see things much more clearly – both of which will make the shift easier. Here we go!

1. What type of relationship do you *wish* you had with your DIL? Describe it in detail.

2. What qualities would a DIL have in *that* relationship?

3. Which of these qualities does *your* DIL have – even if she doesn't necessarily show them in her relationship with you?

4. What *other* positive qualities does your DIL have?

5. What do you appreciate about all these positive qualities in your DIL?

6. Which of your DIL's positive qualities help you to enjoy her?

7. Based on who you are and who your DIL is, what do you see as the positive aspects of your relationship with your DIL? Describe them in detail.

As promised, to eliminate any uncertainty you may have about how to answer these questions, I want to show you an example of the types of responses a MIL might give. You don't need to write essay-length answers, but your responses should be detailed enough for you to be able to connect some vital dots. Here's the example:

1. What type of relationship do you *wish* you had with your DIL? Describe it in detail.
   In my ideal relationship with my DIL, we'd chat on the phone at times. We'd get together for lunch. We'd be in the kitchen talking with each other about different things that are going on in our lives.

2. What qualities would a DIL have in *that* relationship?
   She would be warm, fun, open, approachable, giving, friendly, bright, caring and loving.

3. Which of these qualities does *your* DIL have – even if she doesn't necessarily show them in her relationship with you?
   She's fun, giving, friendly, bright, caring, open and loving.

4. What *other* positive qualities does your DIL have?
   She's a good mom, and she's thoughtful, concerned about others and compassionate.

6. What do you appreciate about all these positive qualities in your DIL?
   I appreciate that she really is a good person with many wonderful qualities.

7. Which of your DIL's positive qualities help you to enjoy her?
   I enjoy that she's bright, loving, thoughtful and a good mom.

8. Based on who you are and who your DIL is, what do you see as the positive aspects of your relationship with your DIL? Describe them in detail.
   Even though we're not super close, we do have an understanding between us. We seem to value a lot of the same things about people and relationships. She's a person of quality, and I'm proud of who she is.

This should help you to begin seeing your MIL-DIL relationship a bit differently. Once you shift your expectations, you'll be able to feel more relaxed and less concerned about having to make this relationship into something else. Then it can start to unfold more naturally. Whether your DIL feels the calmness and begins to respond positively or whether she remains the same, *you'll* be more at ease. And that will change your perspective of the relationship and will help you to be more consistent with who you are. And *that* in turn will start to show in your actions.

Tool 2: Get To Know Your DIL for Who She Really Is

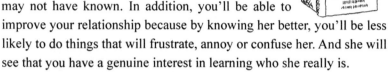

Now that you've shifted your expectations and become more relaxed and comfortable within the relationship, you are in a wonderful position to finally get to know who your DIL really is. In doing so, you'll discover some things about her that you may not have known. In addition, you'll be able to improve your relationship because by knowing her better, you'll be less likely to do things that will frustrate, annoy or confuse her. And she will see that you have a genuine interest in learning who she really is.

For example, do you know if your DIL is the planner type or if she's more impromptu and spontaneous? Do you know the foods your DIL doesn't like as well as the ones she absolutely loves? Is your DIL a shopper, a reader or a crafter? Does she like jewelry and, if so, which kind or style? Does she prefer being in control or going with the flow? What specific brands does she prefer? What organizations does she belong to? What social causes matter to her? I could go on and on with the questions, but I think you get where I'm going here.

What follows are some things you can do both to slowly get to know your DIL better and to help show your DIL that she matters to you – not in a needy, anxious or even self-serving way but more in a you're-an-interesting-person-who-I'd-like-to-get-to-know-better way. And because your expectations are different now, you will feel more relaxed and you will come across as less anxious.

Spend some time learning who your DIL is and what she's all about. Now that the weight of your old expectations has lifted, this might be a good time to take your DIL out to lunch and ask some fairly open-ended questions about what she likes and dislikes, how she feels about certain things and what kinds of things do and don't matter to her. (But remember to keep it casual and friendly – you don't want lunch to feel like the Inquisition.) Or you might invite your DIL to do something with you that you already know she likes to do – and then watch and listen to pick up things about her that you didn't know before. Keep in mind that your son married her because he loves her. See how many of her positive qualities you can discover.

Remember, learning about your DIL is not about *you doing* anything to change the relationship, and it's not about *getting her* to change. It's about *you learning who this woman is* and learning to enjoy her for that alone. No expectations, no pressure.

Find ways that you can be helpful to your DIL. Again, because you are no longer feeling the strain of trying to make a relationship happen, you'll free up more of your energy and you'll behave more consistently. This gives you the chance to show your DIL who *you* really are – and maybe slowly change her perception of you.

Some of the things you could do include volunteering to babysit, picking up the grandchildren from school or from aftercare, helping your DIL prepare for a birthday party and so on. Start slow, and if she turns you down, realize that it may be because of your history of inconsistent behavior. If you are sure this is the case, then preface your request to help with, "I know I've not been very reliable in the past, and I'm sorry for that. I know my actions created a lot of problems for you. I would love a second chance ... ." If you start doing some of these helpful things when there isn't a crisis going on, you will be able to build trust between the two of you. Here's an example of how this can work:

> You know your DIL will be home all day with the kids on both Thursday and Friday of next week. You would like to give her a break for part of the day and allow her a chance to get some things done without having to deal with the kids the whole time. You call her and say, "Hi, Tracy! I know you're home with the kids all day next Thursday and Friday, and I was wondering what you thought about me picking them up on one of those afternoons for a few hours. It would be a great opportunity for me to spend time with them, but also for you to have some free time to do whatever you want. I can work around your schedule, so if that idea sounds good to you, just let me know which day and time would be best."

Notice that in this example, it's not a crisis situation. It is a time when your DIL could just as easily be with her children. By initially choosing non-critical times, you allow her to feel she has some control over things – she has nothing to lose – in case you end up going back to some inconsistent behavior. If you do this on several more occasions, and you're consistent with your follow-through, your Transitioned Tracy will begin to see that she *can* rely on you. And then you'll start to build a relationship based on trust and consistency. Again, since you are no longer looking for a close MIL-DIL bond in your relationship, you can work on creating a relationship of mutual respect and appreciation. Then you can work your way up to helping out in more critical times. For example:

> Your DIL is getting ready to have a gathering of co-workers at her house. You are aware that she's busy making lists of what she needs to do to get things ready. You're not really sure if you can be helpful, but because you've been showing her your ability to follow through with what you say you'll do by helping her out during non-critical times, you see this as an opportunity to build on your relationship.

> You've figured out that your DIL gets a bit short with the children when she's stressed out – it's a lose-lose for all of them. So you say, "Tracy, you seem so busy planning for your upcoming party. Would you like me to take the kids tonight? I could pick them up at whatever time works for you, take them to dinner and then bring them over here to my place for a while. You can just let me know when you'd like me to have them back."

In this example, it is clear the MIL has spent some time not only getting to know her DIL, but because she's already shown her ability to be reliable, she feels ready to test the waters in a more stressful situation. Your Transitioned Tracy may say, "Hey, that's great." Or, she may say, "No, that's OK. I'm fine." And either way is all right because you are still showing her this *new* you.

But what if your DIL and son live too far away to make these steps practical? How do you get to know your DIL then? Obviously, this is much harder, but it can still be done. If you think back, your son probably told you things about your DIL when they were dating, so this will give you at least some information.

Observing your DIL and son together when you do see them is another way to learn about your DIL. Although her actions will be somewhat contrived because of the short time and artificial conditions, you can still take this opportunity to learn a few things about your DIL and her personality. And when you call your son to talk, take some time to talk with your DIL as well. Discuss the kids, her work, her hobbies – anything to get to know her better. Initially, this may be awkward, but that will change before you know it.

You will find that if you practice the tools in this chapter over and over again, you will become more comfortable using them – and in turn, you will become more comfortable with your DIL. As you do so, you'll begin to recognize that you have more influence in the relationship than you ever imagined. You'll also start to see that you and your DIL have more in common than you thought – after all, she's figuring things out about this relationship, just like you; she loves your son, just like you; she doesn't want to make waves or create problems, just like you. Remember, Transitioned Tracy always needs a reason to want to reach out and engage with you – so help her find several!

Chapter 11

When Your MIL Is a Mothering Margaret

Now we're moving on to the tools designed specifically for DILs, starting with those who have Mothering Margaret for their MIL. As you may remember, Mothering Margaret is the MIL who is struggling with her new role in her son's life. She wants to believe she is still *numero uno* with him, and her actions reflect this belief. She typically has strong opinions and feels that sharing those opinions is just being "helpful." And although Margaret doesn't necessarily mother her son in the traditional fashion, often her presence can still come across as quite imposing. What does a DIL do when she has Mothering Margaret for a MIL? Here are a few really good suggestions!

Tool 1: Recognize When the Situation Actually Belongs to You

Mothering Margaret's behavior is a bit trickier to change than that of the other MIL character types because both Margaret *and* her DIL play key roles in the struggle they are experiencing. Remember the discussion in Chapter 2 about how your history and your emotional baggage play a role in why your relationship with your MIL is so hard? Having Margaret as your MIL usually brings up a classic example of this. Let me explain.

As your MIL, Mothering Margaret may stir up feelings inside you that you're stupid, inadequate or otherwise lesser than – or you may simply feel judged or criticized when you're around her. *But Margaret did not create these feelings in you.* They were created long before she ever came into your life. These feelings were initially created in your childhood through many different interactions in many different situations. Granted, Margaret *did* find a way to highlight or reactivate these issues, but the point is that you have felt these feelings many times before your MIL came into the picture. So first, **figure out what is *your* part in these feelings that were stirred up and what is *her* part.**

This step is vital because, as you read in Chapter 7, you don't want to react to what you *perceive* your MIL's intent to be and start that snowball rolling! When you *do* react to Mothering Margaret, you want to base your reaction on *her actions*, not your unique perspective. You want to maintain some objectivity in how you perceive her words or behaviors, which means taking care of your part of the equation so you can react on target to your MIL's behavior.

How do you attain such objectivity? It's not always easy at first, but here's an exercise that will help. Not only will this exercise give you a good sense of what is going on with you when you are having this challenge with your MIL, but it will also shift you away from having the unpleasant feeling when you're with her to begin with. Start by thinking of a time in the past when Mothering Margaret has stirred up this feeling in you, and give the feeling a name (feeling stupid, inadequate, not good enough and so on). Then get a pencil and paper and write down the answers to the following questions. (Writing them down instead of keeping track of them in your head will have a much bigger impact, so it will yield more striking results.) Try to do this exercise *before* you see your MIL again so you will be more prepared when the two of you are together. You will be able to think back to this exercise and be one step ahead. Here we go!

1. What did your MIL do or say that stirred up this feeling inside you?

2. Can you think of one or more situations from your childhood when you also felt like this? Describe it/them.

3. Who was the person in your past who stirred up this feeling in you?

4. How is your MIL like this person – what things about her are similar to this person from your past?

5. What things about your MIL make her different from this person?

Questions 4 and 5 are *critical* to this exercise, so be sure to spend enough time with them to really think your answers through. Then ask yourself:

6. How do these differences between this other person and your MIL make you feel about yourself, and how do they make you see your MIL now?

7. If you weren't stirred up by what your MIL said or did, how might you feel about her actions?

8. Knowing what you know now, how would you probably respond to your MIL?

Now that you are familiar with the questions, take a look at this example of one way a DIL might answer them, as well as how she could use the information she learns to help her interact with her Mothering Margaret MIL.

1. What did your MIL do or say that stirred up this feeling inside you?
   She makes me feel incapable and lesser than.

2. Can you think of one or more situations from your childhood when you also felt like this? Describe it/them.
   It used to be my job to set the table when I was little. When I would start putting things in their place, my mom would go behind me and change where I put things.

3. Who was the person in your past who stirred up this feeling in you?
    My mom.

4. How is your MIL like this person – what things about her are similar to this person from your past?
    They are both picky about how things are done; they are both pretty rigid in their thinking; they are both intimidating to some degree; they are both "take-charge" kind of people.

5. What things about your MIL make her different from this person?
    My MIL laughs more than my mom. I can talk to my MIL about things I could never talk to my mom about. My MIL is very generous, both with her time and with her money. My MIL is always willing to jump in and help.

6. How do these differences between this other person and your MIL make you feel about yourself, and how do they make you see your MIL now?
    In some ways, they make me feel sad for myself. And I feel a little disloyal to my mom. I also feel kind of lucky to have a MIL who really cares.
    Maybe my MIL isn't really as bad as I thought. She's probably a good person who just has some quirky aspects that can get on my nerves. I think she really does like me.

7. If you weren't stirred up by what your MIL said or did, how might you feel about her actions?
    I'd probably feel less emotional. I probably wouldn't take those things so personally.

8. Knowing what you know now, how would you probably respond to your MIL?
    I would probably just think that's her being her. If what she did still bothered me, I could probably say something without it becoming a war.

Now let's take a look at an example of what successfully using this tool could look like:

Your MIL makes a comment to you that initially gets you fuming. However, you sit with your feelings for a moment instead of immediately reacting to what she said. In doing so, you realize that this feeling is one you've had many times and in many different situations with different people. Knowing this almost gives you a sense of relief because you know this is more about *you* than your MIL, which in turn means you can do something about it to help yourself feel better. You start to realize that even though your MIL stirred up this feeling inside you, she is not *trying* to be hurtful or mean. This allows you to see her a bit differently than you did before – maybe more for who she really is. Your initial angry feeling starts to subside, and you are able to react in a way that reflects the situation instead of your old feeling. This entire thought process takes place in less than two minutes.

Things won't necessarily go this smoothly every single time, and you might not always be able to quickly and easily identify the old feelings from your past. But even so, going through this process begins to break the painful cycle of emotions that make you feel so bad about yourself that you end up reacting to the painful emotions instead of to the actual situation at hand. And the more you use this tool, the quicker and easier it will be for you to identify your feelings and put them where they belong.

Tool 2: Establish Your Needs and Wants Without Making Waves

But what happens if the problem really *is* your Mothering Margaret MIL? Believe me, your MIL plays her part in the relationship struggle. She is Mothering Margaret after all! Part of the problem between you and your MIL is that your MIL is so used to being in charge and being in control that it's hard for her to shift out of that role. But the good news is that unlike Off-the-Wall Wanda who has no ability to self-reflect, Margaret is more than willing to look at things and to do what she can to make this a better, smoother relationship.

To help Mothering Margaret truly comprehend how things need to be, it's important that you help her understand clearly what your needs and wants are and what her role is with you and within *your* family. Even though this may sound difficult at first, it's really rather simple. All you have to do is **state what you want from her in a kind, compassionate, and loving way.** Remember – Margaret wants to be included. You matter to her more than you know, so you don't have to be mean or harsh to get your point across. You just need to be *clear*. Here's an example of how this tool works:

> You discover that your MIL came to your house when neither you nor your husband was home. She came inside and set some toys and clothes that your kids left at her house on the counter, along with a note. This drives you crazy. It feels intrusive and creepy, to say the least, and you don't want her to do it again.

> You take some deep breaths and calm yourself down. Then you call your MIL and say, "I appreciate that you brought over the clothes and toys, but I really need you to *do me a favor*. Can you wait until I'm home to bring things over the next time? I know it may seem silly, but I'd really appreciate it if you could do this for me."

A couple of things are at work here. First, you showed your appreciation for your MIL's actions of bringing the clothes and toys to your house. It wasn't the fact that she brought these things over that upset you; it was *when* she brought them over that was the problem. And second, you asked her specifically to do you a favor. After all, when someone asks for a simple favor, it's really hard to say no – don't you think? And again, because you are asking with kindness and compassion and in a loving way, how can she be upset with you? You are not attacking her in any way; you are just stating what you need from her. Here's another example:

Your MIL walks into your house unannounced and uninvited. You're in the middle of folding laundry and getting the kids some lunch before you have to take the oldest one to gymnastics. You find this impromptu visit very irritating, and you really want her to see that stopping by in this way is not a good thing.

Acting surprised, you say to her in a warm, kind voice, "Oh boy, this is a really bad time. I'm right in the middle of finishing up laundry and getting the kids lunch before we have to dash out the door to gymnastics." You continue taking care of what you need to do so you can leave on time, adding, "How about if we plan a time when we can get together for lunch or something? Let me give you a call when I get back and we can schedule it." You make sure to follow through with the call when you get back home, and the two of you end up having lunch later in the week.

But what if you don't deal with it at the time because the situation was either too uncomfortable for you or because your Mothering Margaret just caught you so off guard? Cut yourself some slack. It's really OK because you can always go back and address it later – whether in person or on the phone. The truth is that it's never too late.

Here's a trick for going back and fixing it later. Whenever you think of a better way to handle a situation with Margaret after the fact, all you have to say initially is, "You know, I was thinking about what happened earlier and ..." or "I was thinking about what you said and ... ." Let's take a look at how that might play out in the above example:

After you get home from taking your child to gymnastics, you call your MIL and say, "You know, I've been thinking about what happened earlier, and I feel really bad that I couldn't visit with you the way I wanted to. You just caught us at such a bad time, and I felt I had to rush you out the door. So could you do me a favor and call me first – before you come over? Then I can let you know if it's a good time or if we're in the middle of something. You would be doing me *such* a favor and that way when you do come over, I'll have time to sit and talk with you."

You may be thinking that you can't say these things to your MIL. It's not easy when you're not used to asking her to get your needs met! But with your MIL as well as with anyone else in your life, learning to let others know what you need from them is important. Remember, no one – not even your MIL – is a mind reader, and most people will be willing to accommodate you if they know what it is that you want from them.

Even if both of these tools initially seem awkward and difficult, it's important to get into the habit of using both of them. The more you do, the more comfortable they will feel and the better results you will achieve. Trust me, the initial effort will be *more* than worth it the first time you end up saying to yourself, *Wow!* That *was easy! Why didn't I ever think to try that before?*

Chapter 12

When Your MIL Is an Off-the-Wall Wanda

This chapter is devoted to helping DILs deal with Off-the-Wall Wanda. I am sure you remember this MIL character. With her extreme, insensitive, self-centered behavior, Wanda is pretty hard to forget! She can make the blood pressure of even the most confident, even-keeled DIL start to rise.

Even though Wanda is the most challenging type of MIL to deal with, she *can* be dealt with. But for the best results, you must remember to keep two vital points in mind. First, *never take anything Wanda says or does personally.* I know that's hard to do, but it will be easier if you remember that she treats *everyone* this same way and that her behavior is much more about *her* than it is about *you.*

Second, remember that *this is probably going to be a slow process.* Keep in mind that the big shifts in behavior required with Wanda take time and usually occur in baby steps. So the first few times you use these tools, you may see only a small change or maybe even no change at all! But stick with the tools presented here because if you keep using them, you *will* eventually see results. So let's get started!

Tool 1: Set Firm, Clear Boundaries

This tool sounds easier than it actually is because typically, the people who have to deal with Off-the-Wall Wanda are nice, kind, thoughtful people who don't want to make anyone around them feel uncomfortable or uneasy in any way. But when dealing with someone like Wanda, you have to set boundaries that you don't usually have to set because unlike most people, Wanda does not have a good understanding of what is and is not acceptable behavior.

Wanda's behavior can easily catch you off guard because at first, you won't even realize you need to set boundaries until Wanda starts trampling all over them. In all honesty, your mind just doesn't think in those terms. But when you're dealing with Wanda, you have to *train yourself not to take boundaries for granted and to always keep that need in the back of your mind.* This will take practice and a conscious effort, so keep reminding yourself.

Realizing you need to set boundaries is one thing, but actually setting them is quite another. In the beginning, when your MIL catches you off guard and you stumble and fumble, it's OK. These occasions will only reinforce why you need to set boundaries in the first place. Rest assured that the process will get easier as time goes on, and eventually you'll become a boundary-setting pro.

You have one advantage here, right off the bat, because some of Wanda's outrageous behaviors are predictable. For example, she may *always* expect you and your family to attend *all* family get-togethers – for the duration of the event. Or she may consistently barrage you with questions or her opinions if she doesn't agree with something you've said or done. Or she may make a habit of keeping you on the phone for what seems like hours – as she talks but never listens. No matter what her outrageous behavior is, you can often predict how she's going to act. So that's the place to start. **The most important thing to keep in mind when you set boundaries is that while you can be nice, always be firm – no wavering or hesitation.** Here's an example of how this works:

When your MIL calls, she can keep you on the phone for what seems like hours talking about nothing. You try being polite. You listen, trying to interject, yet you find yourself doing other things while you're talking (or rather listening) to her. It's gotten to the point that you check the caller ID before you answer the phone, just so you can avoid her if possible. Although you really don't like doing this, you don't know what else to do. Eventually, you decide you must set a boundary with her.

So the next time your MIL calls, you decide you are willing to talk with her for 10 minutes – at the very most 15. Before she can start jabbering, you say, "Oh, hi, Wanda. I'm so sorry I only have 10 minutes to talk, so I'll have to keep it short ... ." And then you let her talk. You don't give her a reason for the time limit; you just establish your boundary. After 10 minutes, she's still talking away. So you interrupt her and interject, "Sorry to interrupt you Wanda, but I really need to go now. These 10 minutes have just flown by, haven't they? We'll talk again soon." And then you hang up the phone.

The trick to making this work is that you don't wait for Wanda to agree, react, respond, say goodbye or even say anything at all. After the time limit is up and you mention that fact, *you just hang up.* If you linger on the phone for even a short period of time, Wanda will hook you right back into remaining on the phone with her, which is what she wants. Remember, Wanda wants what she wants when she wants it. It is never about you. And that means that you cannot reason with her. You can only demonstrate what you need through your behavior and through being firm about keeping the boundaries you set.

I should warn you that initially, Wanda will do whatever it takes to make you feel guilty in hopes that you will revert to your old, easy-to-manipulate behavior. However, if you stick to your boundaries, in time she will really get that when you say something you mean it. She'll eventually understand that, for example, *10 minutes means 10 minutes.*

Of course, your stomach will probably be in knots when you do this. (In fact, it's probably in knots just reading this example!) You'll most likely feel as though you're being rude, mean, insensitive or even disrespectful – but you're not. The truth is that your MIL sets you up to behave this way with her.

Because of her lack of self-discipline and her inability to play within the commonly accepted social rules, Wanda puts the responsibility of setting limits or setting boundaries on the people around her. But they usually let her do whatever she wants because they don't want to *feel* as though they are being rude in any way. Once you learn to set clear, firm boundaries, however, this dynamic will change for good!

Tool 2: Make Good Use of Humor

As predictable as some of Wanda's actions can be, she can also be equally *un*predictable – particularly with the words she chooses to use. Nothing is worse than being constantly left with your mouth hanging open whenever you interact with her. You may well end up beating yourself up for not having a snappy comeback, or maybe you say to yourself, *I can't believe she did it again.* But no matter how well you prepare yourself, Wanda always seems to get the upper hand.

The best way to deal with Wanda's unpredictable comments is to use humor. **Humor works because it shifts the power balance within the relationship.** It catches your MIL off guard and you immediately gain the upper hand – and yet at the same time, you're being nice, funny and lighthearted. It will be hard for Wanda to come back at you with some crazy comment or action because you are making it clear that you are not offended by her comment. Here's an example of how this works:

Your MIL doesn't always agree with how you're raising your kids. One day, she says, "Maybe the kids should have some chores to do so they can learn about responsibility. They never do anything around here."

Laughing, you respond by saying, "You're right, Wanda. At this rate, they'll be living with us until they are 50 years old. I can see the headlines in the paper now: *Adult Children Left on Their Own Without Adequate Supervision After Mother Dies. All Siblings Perish.* " You continue to laugh as you say this, and then in a lighthearted manner, you quickly change the subject. Or if there is someone else around, you immediately start talking with this other person, shaking your head, but as if your MIL never uttered her caustic comment.

Another way to respond is to **simply laugh**. Laugh out loud with that I'm-in-on-this-joke kind of laugh. Don't laugh in a mean way, of course, but in a way that says you think Wanda is being funny and that you are being a good sport. Laughter sends a message that no words ever can. Here's an example:

Your MIL is at your house for dinner. Everyone is sitting around enjoying the food and conversation until Wanda asks you loudly enough for everyone to hear, "Are you gaining weight? You look a little chubbier than you did the last time I saw you." So you start laughing as though she's the funniest comedienne around. As you continue to laugh, you start to shake your head, and then you slow the laughter down until you're merely chuckling – and at that point, you begin talking to someone else as if Wanda never said anything.

By bringing humor and laughter into the situation, you will be disarming your Off-the-Wall Wanda and the situation, yet you will be doing so in a non-threatening way. You will be redirecting the power in the relationship away from Wanda and establishing yourself as the one in control. This is a subtle but effective strategy. Not only will you feel empowered, but you will also help everyone else in the room feel more at ease with the situation. And believe me, they will appreciate that!

Another good strategy for dealing with unpredictable comments is to **prepare in advance by having some generic phrases that you can toss off whenever you need them**, always using a twist of humor as you do so. The phrases can be something as simple as *"Really?"* (said in an incredulous tone), "Oh my gosh, I can't believe that just flew out of your mouth" or "Did you just say _____?" (as you repeat back to Wanda what she just said in an innocent, confused, did-I-hear-you-right tone). Here's an example:

> The extended family is taking a short vacation together at a rented cottage. Your MIL knows that you are planning to run a marathon and that you've been working with a trainer to get ready. She knows that you have been running just about every day as part of your preparation. Although you've been running while you've been at the cottage, you haven't been training as hard as you do at home.

> This morning, it's raining and cold. You've decided you will wait for the rain to stop before you go out for your run. You're sitting at the kitchen table drinking a cup of coffee when Wanda screeches from across the room, "I thought you were training for a marathon! Aren't you going out running today? Or are you slacking off while you're here?"

> You laugh as you reply, "Did you just ask me if I'm slacking off because I'm not out running in this storm?" Then you shake your head in a good-natured way, as if you can't believe how funny your MIL is, and you go back to what you were doing before she made the comment.

By speaking up and casually, even comically, challenging Off-the-Wall Wanda's words, you will be taking her thunder away. She will no longer have one up on you. And at the same time, you will be letting her know that what she's saying is not OK. Although you'll be doing this nicely, your message is loud and clear.

Both of these tools will undoubtedly help empower you in the face of what has seemed in the past like an impossible situation. As you practice and become more adept at the tools, you will actually find it easier to be around Wanda because you will feel that you can deal with anything she throws at you. Not only will this boost your confidence around handling your MIL, but also you will ultimately feel better about yourself. You may never look forward to spending time with Wanda, but trust me, your encounters will no longer remind you of having a root canal without an anesthetic.

Chapter 13

When Your MIL Is an Uncertain Sara

This chapter is for any DIL whose MIL is Uncertain Sara. As you may remember, Uncertain Sara has done a pretty good job of carving out a life for herself beyond that of being a mom, and she feels good about that. She likes her DIL and is happy that her son has found someone he loves.

Yet Sara struggles with what her relationship with her DIL is supposed to look like. She's unsure of what her new role should be and how she should interact. Although she tries several different things in an attempt to find what feels right, her uncertainty feeds her anxiety, resulting in some awkward interactions. Uncertain Sara may try too hard, for example, or she may just seem a bit off. And although her actions truly are harmless, the bottom line is that she makes it difficult to have a relationship with her. So what can a DIL do to help smooth the way when her MIL is Uncertain Sara? Here are a few tools that work wonders.

Tool 1: Harness the Power of the Inside Joke

The first thing to remind yourself about Sara is that even though her actions can be irritating, she really is harmless. She just doesn't think, and her anxiety can get the better of her. And because it really is true that she means no harm, her actions can be rather funny when you think about them. When your husband sees her in the same way that you do (as a bit off at times, but well meaning), then the two of you can laugh and joke together about her words or actions. You might give each other a certain look from across the room, for example, or nudge one another under the table and then flash a knowing smile between you. However you choose to do it, harnessing the power of the inside joke makes most of these potentially stressful situations with your MIL OK – and even funny (in a head-shaking, I-don't-believe-she-just-said/did-that kind of way). Take a look at this example:

Your MIL has heard everyone rave about your double chocolate cake. She's also watched people devour it at family get-togethers while her desserts just seem to sit there, barely touched. The family will be getting together for another big event soon, and you ask Sara what she'd like you to bring. First, she says, "Oh, you really don't need to bring anything. I'm just putting a few things together." Then mentioning her daughters, Sara adds, "And Susie and Alice will be bringing some dishes, too."

As you speak with her further about the get-together, you realize that she's really having quite a feast. You again mention that you'd like to contribute and that since everything else seems to be covered, you suggest you bring a dessert. Sara immediately replies, "You know, I have dessert covered. Why don't you bring some bread or rolls?"

Bread or rolls? you think to yourself. *Are you kidding me? Really?* But you tell Sara that you'll be happy to bring some rolls.

When you and your husband arrive at the family get-together, you place your rolls in a basket on the table. Sara comments on how wonderful they look. You and your husband just look at each other and chuckle. And then you both glance at the table of desserts across the room. You look at each other, shake your heads and smile. The table of desserts consists of – a single plate of cookies.

In this example, you and your husband are on the same page with the way you view Uncertain Sara's words and actions. And because you view the situation the same way, and because you both know that Sara wasn't trying to hurt you or make you feel frustrated, **you can use the inside joke as a way to let off a little steam**.

I'm not saying that Sara's actions don't sometimes annoy you – because they probably do. But this annoyance is not so strong that it significantly affects you. So you can afford to make light of it. What's more, unlike the humor tool suggested for dealing with Off-the-Wall Wanda, the humor used with Uncertain Sara is not something she witnesses directly. With Sara, the humor stays between you and your husband.

Tool 2: Examine Your Husband's Role, as Well as Your Own Role

But what if you don't find Uncertain Sara's behavior all that humorous? Let's say she tries *overly* hard and it gets on your nerves too much to have a comfortable relationship with her. Or maybe her uncertainty or anxiety comes out in such a way that you can't depend on her when you need to. What do you do then?

When you can't find Sara's words or her behavior the least bit humorous, examine whether or not you and your husband are really on the same page. Look to see if he might be somehow playing into the scenario; in other words, is he:

- defensive about his mother?

- acting as if he's caught in the middle between the two of you?

- acting as if he doesn't understand your issues with her?

- contributing to the problem in other ways, such as avoiding hearing your side or dismissing his mother's actions with a comment like, "That's just my mom. Don't let it bother you"?

The truth is that **when your husband is *not* on the same page as you are about his mother, you feel as though you're fighting two people, not just one.** And this makes you feel so much more alone with what is going on than you would feel if he understood how you experience his mother. If you find that your husband *is* a contributing factor, you will need to follow a two-step process. Let me walk you through both parts.

First, acknowledge your feelings (to yourself), whether you're feeling hurt, angry, frustrated or simply justified in seeing him as a jerk. After all, it's exhausting enough to have to deal with your husband's mother, but when you add *him* to the mix – well, it's understandable if it seems like a lot to handle.

As important as it is for you to acknowledge and really feel your feelings, do this by yourself, away from your husband, because sharing those feelings of frustration and anger with him will not make things better. In fact, it will make things worse. And here's why: If you share these feelings, even if you're justified in having them, your husband will focus only on *how* you're coming across (like an emotional crazy lady) instead of hearing the message behind your emotion. So instead of discussing *his* role in the tensions between you and his mother, the two of you will instead end up arguing about *your* yelling, *your* irrational behavior, *your* over-exaggerating, *your* hypersensitivity and on and on. As you can imagine, not only does that *not* help the situation, but you will also end up feeling more alone than ever.

So just don't go there. Feel you feelings – get them all out. And then take a few deep breaths to calm yourself down because if you want him to really hear you and not get defensive and upset, you must approach him calmly.

Then (and only then) you are ready for the second step – taking a look at how his actions are affecting you, what you want from him, and what stops you from getting that. *How do I do that?* you may well be wondering. The easiest way is to ask yourself what you are doing or saying that may be contributing to his being defensive, avoiding the issues altogether, or displaying whatever behavior is making you feel so alone in the situation. Here is an example:

Transitioned Tracy is struggling with her MIL, Uncertain Sara. Sara just wears Tracy out with her chatter, her inconsistent behavior and her attempt to try to connect with her in ways that make Tracy less than eager to do so. Tracy's not really interested in having a relationship with Sara, but Sara keeps pushing for it to happen. Tracy has tried talking to her husband about this, but that seems to go nowhere.

Tracy decides to think this through a bit to see if she can figure out what is going on. She realizes she needs to do a process of elimination to figure out exactly who's doing what. She decides to start with her husband and see if he is playing any part in this, and then she will look at herself. As she begins to go through the questions and situations that pertain to her husband, she hits the jackpot. *Aaaauuughhh!* she thinks to herself. *Now it makes so much sense why we fight about his mother the way we do – and why that makes me dislike her even more. He acts like his mother's behavior is not a problem because he feels so uncomfortable about the tension between us. So he dismisses what I say as though I'm making too big a deal about what she's said or done. I knew she was being difficult, but now I see that he's being difficult, too!*

Tracy is totally steeped in her feelings. She's finding it difficult to contain herself, but she works really hard to keep the lid on her emotions. She knows saying something to her husband at this point would only cause a fight. She spends the next few hours thinking and feeling – working through her emotions until she is calm enough to talk with her husband without blowing up at him. She is willing to take the time and effort because she really wants to get this straightened out once and for all, and she knows she needs to stay focused on what she wants to accomplish. She also knows that to do this she needs to take a good, hard look at what *she* may be doing or saying that is causing her husband to react in the irritating and unhelpful way he does.

Although this is not easy for her, she sticks with it until – *Ugh!* There it is. She begins to see that when she talks to her husband about his mother, and her voice rises with every breath she takes, what her body language and her voice inflection are actually telling him is, "I know I'm right. You will *never* convince me that your mother is *anything* but a huge pain!" Yikes! This is a real eye-opener for her. Tracy really had no idea that she was coming across so forcefully. After all, in her thinking, she's just trying to make her point.

Tracy takes a few more deep breaths as she tries to figure out what to do next. *OK,* she thinks, *I need to remember what my goal is here and what I need to do or say to help me get closer to it.* She's ready to make some changes in her own behavior so that her husband will feel able to shift his behavior, too, putting them on the same page more often.

If this sounds a bit familiar it's because it's the same kind of idea you were looking at in Chapter 7 about perception (or misperception) and reactions with your MIL. But now, these issues involve your husband. So let's look at the same sorts of questions – but this time worded from the perspective of dealing with your husband.

Perception Exercise for DILs About Their Husbands

Think about a situation with your husband when his response to something you said or did about his mother wasn't ideal. Then write down your answers to the following questions:

1. What behavior did you display or what did you say that upset your husband?

2. When you did or said this thing, how did your husband react or respond to you? For example: Did he ignore you, discount your feelings about the situation with his mother, dismiss what you said or defend his mother?

3. Considering the different types of husbands (see Chapter 5 if you need a refresher), think for a moment how someone who is like an In-the-Middle Michael would interpret or perceive your behavior. Then think about how a Struggling Steven would interpret that same behavior. Now, thinking about which character your husband is like most of the time, how would someone who is *that type* perceive the *behavior* you displayed or the words you said?

4. When you said or did whatever it was, what was your intention at the time?

5. How could you do or say things differently to help your husband perceive you more accurately?

Reaction Exercise for DILs About Their Husbands

Think about an interaction you had with your husband about his mother when your feelings were stirred up. Then write down your answers to the following questions:

1. What feeling was stirred up inside you?

2. When you felt this way, how did this feeling show in your behavior (for example, did you feel yourself attacking more with your words, putting up walls or yelling louder)?

3. If someone else – a friend or an acquaintance – behaved the same way toward you as you behaved toward your husband, how would you feel?

4. How would you then react to that person?

5. How did your husband react or respond to your behavior?

6. How could your behavior be directly related to your husband's reaction?

OK, now let's say you've eliminated your husband's part of the problem, if any, and yet Uncertain Sara's words or actions still have a big impact on you. What *then*? **Ask yourself,** *Why do I let my MIL bother me so much?* **and** *How might my expectations of my MIL be adding to the problem?*

Many of you may be thinking, *But I don't* have *expectations of my MIL.* Well, let me just say that if Uncertain Sara bothers you or still upsets you, then the truth is that you most likely *do* have expectations of her because, otherwise, why does she bother you so much? This may sound like circular logic, but look at it this way. If you really don't have expectations of someone, then that person's actions (good or bad) would not really have any impact on you. You might feel some mild displeasure or even a bit of an annoyance, but it wouldn't be anything that would really affect you one way or the other.

In any case, if you realize that your MIL still bothers you to some degree, you basically have two choices: You can either figure out why you still have expectations of her and address those expectations, or you can just accept the fact that she still bothers you *and* the fact that you have expectations. If your choice is the latter, then you'll find the next tool very useful.

Tool 3: Establish Your MIL's Role Within *Your* Family

If your Uncertain Sara MIL can't figure out her role with you, then take the initiative and let her know what *you* see her role to be. This works to your advantage because it puts you in the driver's seat as far as what you want and need from Sara. But before you start visualizing her role, it's important to first determine what role you and your husband *really* want your MIL to play in your family. And to do that, the two of you need to think about who she is. In other words, is your MIL someone you can:

- ask a favor of – and she'll follow through?
- chat with only periodically?
- invite over for dinner? Or is it better to go out to dinner when you're with her?
- feel comfortable visiting with for a long weekend or a week? Or is two days plenty of time?
- feel comfortable asking to babysit your children?

Once you are clear about who your MIL is, you and your husband are in a position to decide how important a role you want her to play in your family's life. For example, if she is someone you cannot depend on, then be clear with yourself that you *will not* ask for your MIL's help in those really important times because it sets you up for an emotional drama that you really don't need. Instead, ask for her help only when the outcome is not critical or only when you have a backup plan.

Maybe your MIL tries too hard or is too standoffish. Then you need to be specific about what you want from her so there's no way she can misunderstand what you are trying to say. Use phrases like *I need, I want* or *I wish*. This also helps you to be clear with what you want from her. Let's look at an example:

Your MIL, Sara, seems to be all over the place. One minute she's trying to help you to the point of smothering you; the next she's nowhere to be found when you need her. At other times, she so quiet and passive that you feel as if you're pulling teeth just to get her to commit to something. She's driving you crazy, and you really want to do something about it.

Your daughter is having a soccer banquet at the end of next week. It's a really big deal, and you know your daughter will be receiving at least one big award. A dinner will follow the award presentation, and you have to tell the coach how many people in your family will attend. In the past, when you've tried to ask Sara if she wants to join the family for an event like this, she either has been evasive or has changed her mind at the last minute. So this time you decide to do something a bit different.

You call Sara and say, "Hi Sara. Jody has a soccer banquet next Friday at 5:30 p.m. It includes awards and dinner, and I know Jody will be getting one of the big awards. We would love to have you come with us, but they need to know how many of us will be attending. *I need* you to let me know by Monday evening whether or not you are coming so I can call them Tuesday morning with our count. So if I don't hear from you by Monday evening, I will assume you're not coming. But do check your calendar because we'd really love you to be there to see Jody get her award."

Uncertain Sara now knows exactly what you need from her and when you need it. And because you've avoided creating a situation where you'll be pulling your hair out if Sara doesn't get back to you on time, you sound much more relaxed than usual, so your invitation sounds much more genuine. That in turn makes Sara feel less apprehensive and uncertain, so she will be less likely to have a problem getting back to you on time. Also, if Sara has a tendency to say she'll go but then actually back out at the last minute, anticipate that possibility. If it does happen, then no one in the family will be surprised. Sara's backing out at the last minute can be a running family joke – "Grandma Sara says she's coming, *but we all know what that means!*" In either case, everyone wins!

If the situation involves a financial issue, where you must pay in advance for something, then by all means let her know that if she says she'll attend, you'll be buying her ticket ahead of time. By doing this, you are letting her know that if she says she wants to attend, she's not just making a commitment to you and your family that she'll be there, she's also committing your family's money.

A huge benefit to using this tool is that when you help your MIL establish her role within your family, you help her know where she fits. And this allows her to be less anxious and so act in less irritating ways. This goes a long way in shaping the MIL-DIL relationship into something that works for both of you.

Part IV:

Finishing Touches

Chapter 14

We've Come a Long Way, Baby!

Now that you've made it through most of this book, you finally have some answers to those nagging questions you've been carrying around about your in-law. You have new concepts to help you think about your in-law *and* yourself a bit differently. And you have new tools that you can use to start shifting this relationship in the direction that feels better. Bravo!

I know I've given you a lot to think about and digest, and I've also given you a lot of tasks – including both self-reflection exercises and tools to implement. But they're not just busywork. There's a method to this madness. I've learned through years of experience that people tend to buy self-help books, read them, stick them on a shelf and remain passive participants. They devour every page, feel the information speaks directly to them, highlight or underline the parts that seem the most powerful, yet never really use or practice the tasks or tools that the books outline. *And then they wonder why things are not changing in their relationship.*

If you really want to feel better about your MIL or DIL and have a better relationship with her, it is imperative that you actively use the material provided here. I'm not saying it will be easy, nor am I saying things will change fast; what I *am* saying is that nothing will change if you don't start doing something differently. Providing you with the concepts, tasks and tools that *I know* work is my gift to you. It is my desire that each of you is able to transform your MIL-DIL relationship into one that feels good and adds joy to your life. Having been on both sides of this picture, I know how important and rewarding transforming this relationship really is. So please, be willing to step out of your comfort zone – and practice, practice, practice. That is the only way these tools will become second nature to you. Be willing to take a fearless look at yourself, change those things within yourself that can help you transform this relationship, and remember throughout the entire process that *you have more power to make a difference than you realize.*

An Important Caveat

I do want to mention that there are MILs and DILs who are struggling in many other areas of their lives, beyond the MIL-DIL relationship. If you think this pertains to you, then ask yourself the following questions: Are you (or your in-law) experiencing generalized irritation, not wanting to interact with people in general, feeling a need to sleep a lot, easily angered or easily tearful, or losing interest in things you enjoy? These are a few of the many symptoms of depression.

If this describes you or your in-law, getting professional help is imperative. With depression, things will *not* get better on their own – in fact, *they will get worse.* The combination of medication *and* psychotherapy can create life-changing results that make the difference between feeling alive and feeling as though you are in a fog or cloud of negativity. If you want to find out more about this, you can contact your local mental health community (by looking under "mental health facilities" in your local phone listings), ask your family physician for a referral or visit the Web site for the National Institute of Mental Health, www.nimh.nih.gov/health/publications/depression/complete-index.shtml.

Michelle and Me Today

As you may remember from the story of my Thanksgiving From Hell in the first chapter, my DIL Michelle and I have had some "moments" together. As I mentioned in that chapter, this was not the first incident where we perceived situations so differently that neither of us could see beyond our own pain. Sad to say, that was only one of many such incidents; we both experienced this kind of pain from one another for more than eight years.

Even during those rough years, we did indeed seem to get along at times. We talked, laughed and shared touching moments. But then something would happen, and the closeness that we started to feel and the connection that seemed to be there vanished. Gone. And even though we didn't always have verbal exchanges like the one I described in the Thanksgiving story, tensions between us rose and the connection was broken – and we both felt it.

You may be wondering, *If she's a psychotherapist, why didn't she know how to fix this? Why didn't she fix her relationship sooner instead of letting it go on for so many years?* The truth is that I didn't know how. I knew there was a problem – what an understatement! I just didn't know what to do about it. As skilled a psychotherapist as I am, I was not able to get out of my own way long enough to figure things out.

But I knew I had to do something. This was my son's wife, a woman he loved deeply. And she was someone whom I *used* to get along with and truly loved and cared for dearly. And then there were my grand-daughters, who mean everything to me, getting caught in the middle. I wanted a relationship with *all* of them, and I knew it was up to me – it was my place – to figure this out and to try to turn things around.

As a professional, I began to do the research that resulted in this book. And as I did so, I realized I wasn't alone in my struggles and that the MIL-DIL relationship has unique challenges. When I set out interviewing MILs and DILs, I experienced my first *aha!* moments. As I sat with MILs and DILs, I had both my researcher and psychotherapist hats on. I listened to their stories and asked them questions, and at times when they talked about different instances with themselves and their in-laws, I found myself thinking, *Ooh, that probably wasn't a good idea.* Or I'd find myself catching my breath, thinking, *Wow! That must have done some damage.* But then, as they talked further, my thoughts went to, *Yikes! I do that!* Or, *Oh my gosh! That sounds like* me! Let me tell you, these revelations were not pretty – necessary, yes, but definitely not pretty.

I found myself sitting with these realizations for a long time, really taking in what I was learning about my relationship with Michelle and about myself. And then things started coming together for me. Once I discovered the different MIL-DIL patterns that people fell into, I began to see the individual characters unfold within the patterns. I immediately realized I could borrow some of the concepts, strategies and techniques I was using with my clients in psychotherapy to use in my own life with my DIL. After all, these different types of people I was finding among MILs, DILs and husbands/sons were people we've all dealt with at different times in our lives. The solutions I had devised could help just about anyone struggling with an in-law issue – even me!

I definitely recognized myself as one of the MIL characters. To be honest, I initially saw myself as Comfortable Carla, although I soon realized that my DIL probably saw me more as Mothering Margaret. (Again, this is about how *your in-law* perceives you, *not* how you perceive yourself.) And I could see how she might perceive me that way; after all I am a strong, independent woman with definite opinions.

I began using some of the tools that work for the Doubting Donnas, and I took a look at how Mothering Margaret's behavior comes across. Yikes! What an eye-opener that was! But in doing this, I started to shift my feelings about Michelle, our relationship and myself. This began my transformation. This is when changing my behavior made sense to me.

What I've learned over the years as a psychotherapist is that people have to integrate the intellectual *why* with the emotional *aha!* of what they're doing before their behavior can *really* change. It was no different for me. And although I wasn't perfect every time with my new behaviors, I stuck with it. Moreover, I didn't do them just once or twice. I did them whenever the situation arose to use them. I tried as best I could to put my agenda or my goal of transforming this relationship out of my mind and just focus on how these new behaviors that I was demonstrating felt to me. I reminded myself of how much better they made me feel than what I was doing before. As difficult as this was at times, this internal shift is what made me persevere and trust the process.

As I was working on myself, doing much self-reflection and changing my perspective of situations and my behavior, Michelle began to soften. I noticed that slowly, her behavior was changing.

They were small changes, but changes just the same. We didn't share with one another what we each were feeling, what we were noticing about the other or anything about what was happening between us. We both kept our insights, revelations and our own internal shifts to ourselves – probably because we were afraid to bring up anything that might lead us right down into another black hole. But announced or not, shift happened.

I started sharing my intent, for example. I began asking Michelle for her thoughts about something before I acted. I tried to determine if my way was *really* necessary. And sometimes, I'd just take a step back and let her shine. Although at first I didn't see much change in her, I eventually recognized a bit of melting on her part. She seemed just a little less angry with me, a little less tense. And when I experienced that, I found myself able to warm up to her a bit, too. Although I was still cautious, as I'm sure she was with me, I found that I couldn't help myself. When someone treats you with warmth, even if it's just a little, and that person really matters to you, you can't help but reciprocate, right?

Please keep in mind that all this occurred while I lived in Michigan and Michelle lived in Tennessee. I think when you live some distance away from each other, working on your relationship requires even more creativity and commitment because you have such limited time to try new things and to practice. I had to take every opportunity I could find, whether while visiting or talking on the phone.

Whenever I called my son, for example, I always made a point of talking with Michelle, even if it was just for a few minutes. There may have been times when she avoided me – I really can't say, but I worked hard not to let that be where my thoughts would go. We both continued in this dance – shifting, changing, adjusting – for quite some time. Eventually we could both feel *and trust* that something really good was happening between us. We both knew that our relationship was growing and evolving into something that we both could enjoy. A huge weight was lifted for both of us.

Today, both Michelle and I appreciate our relationship in a way we never could before. We continue to grow and evolve as individuals as well as in our relationship with each other. Again, everything is not perfect between us. We stumble sometimes, and occasionally we fall, but the major difference now is that we allow each other to be human – mistakes and all.

About a year or so after my relationship with Michelle began turning around, it underwent yet another change. My husband, Roger, and I moved from Michigan to Tennessee to be closer to Michelle and Anthony. For years, in spite of the problems Michelle and I had been having, we had all talked about Roger and me eventually making such a move when we retired from our current careers. Even though Michelle and I were struggling with our feelings about one another, we both wanted to have a better sense of family, particularly for her children. Because neither Anthony nor Michelle had any family who lived remotely close to them, the idea of having family (either his or hers) nearby appealed to them. And having a chance to be around our granddaughters meant the world to Roger and me. So the inevitable became reality, and fortunately Michelle and I were in a really good place with each other when it all came together.

While we're all glad to be living in the same town now, it's also true that the move brought new challenges to both Michelle and me. We have had to figure out what it means to live close to one another and how that works when all we've ever known is a long-distance relationship. So now we are facing new challenges and making new adjustments, but we're at least going into this with our eyes wide open – and with some incredibly helpful new skills, as well.

A Final Note

Actively pursuing changes in your MIL-DIL relationship is scary, yet necessary if you want your relationship to feel better. You are part of an extended family now. How you see and feel about yourself plays a large part in how you experience the other people in your family. Although you don't have control over anyone else's actions, you do have total control over how *you* feel about them and how *you* react – *that's the key to this whole book*. And by changing how you perceive your in-law's words and actions and making some changes in your own behavior, you can't help but begin to experience this relationship differently. Believe me, you can do it! *Trust the process.*

Appendix: Questionnaires and Scoring Keys

In this appendix, you'll find two questionnaires – one for MILs to use to identify which DIL character they are dealing with and one for DILs to use to identify which MIL character they have. Let me just say upfront that it's pretty much impossible that your MIL or DIL will fit all or even most of the situations outlined in these questions. So don't check each one – no matter how frustrated you are with your in-law! Instead, you'll find that certain questions really do pertain to you and your situation more than others.

It is vital that you take your time here. Think about what each question is asking and how much each one applies or doesn't apply to you and your MIL or DIL. If you believe an answer fits *most* of the time (not just sometimes), then check it. Otherwise, let it go.

After you have completed your questionnaire, look at the scoring key that immediately follows it. This will show you which questions fit with which different MIL or DIL characters. If most of the questions you checked fall into one category, then this is the MIL or DIL character you deal with most of the time. Sometimes, however, you will have *almost* the same number of responses in two different categories. When this happens, you're mostly dealing with the character who has the *highest* number of responses. But the other character will also be present at times, too, so pay attention to the descriptions of *both* characters as you read the chapters. Don't let this double-duty confuse you. As I've mentioned before, everyone is constantly evolving and not every MIL or DIL will fit neatly into a box, so it's quite possible for someone to have characteristics of more than one of these character types.

Here's an example for MILs trying to identify their DILs:

Let's say you chose nine questions that fall under Doubting Donna, five questions that fall under Weird Wendy and four questions that fall under Transitioned Tracy. Your DIL would be a Doubting Donna most of the time.

or

If you chose 12 questions that fall under Doubting Donna, 10 questions that fall under Weird Wendy and six questions that fall under Transitioned Tracy, then your DIL would be a Doubting Donna most of the time, but she also would have some tendencies that belong to Weird Wendy.

but

If you chose exactly the same number of questions that fall under each of two characters, then your DIL might fluctuate between both of them, so give them equal weight when reading the tools.

Similarly, here's an example for DILs trying to identify their MILs:

Let's say you chose 10 questions that fall under Mothering Margaret, six questions that fall under Off-the-Wall Wanda and four questions that fall under Uncertain Sara. Then your MIL would be Mothering Margaret most of the time.

or

If you chose eight questions that fall under Mothering Margaret, 12 questions that fall under Off-the-Wall Wanda and 14 questions that fall under Uncertain Sara, then your MIL would be Uncertain Sara most of the time, but she would also have some tendencies that belong to Off-the-Wall Wanda.

but

If you chose exactly the same number of questions that fall under each of two characters, then your MIL might fluctuate between both of them, so give them equal weight when reading the tools.

By the way, you'll sometimes see an answer listed as belonging to more than one character's category in the scoring key. Don't worry – it's not a misprint! This happens because behaviors typically fall on a continuum, from mild to extreme. A Weird Wendy or an Off-the-Wall Wanda, for example, will display the same basic behavior in very different degrees of severity than would a Doubting Donna or a Mothering Margaret. And the intent behind the behavior will be different, as well. Consequently, the scoring key allows for a behavior with a somewhat broad description to have a slightly different twist, depending on who is displaying it. So don't let that throw you when you go to score your answers.

Ready? Choose the appropriate questionnaire from the next few pages and get started!

Questionnaire for MILs Identifying Their DIL

Please check the statements that *best* fit how you feel or that *best* fit your situation with your DIL.

1. ❏ Does it feel as though you're biting your tongue more often than not when you're around your DIL?

2. ❏ Does your DIL perceive you so negatively that you are at a loss as to where her perception comes from and what to do about it?

3. ❏ Do you try different approaches to engage your DIL, to no avail?

4. ❏ Do you feel as though your DIL completely misunderstands you?

5. ❏ Do you feel on edge around your DIL, as if you're not sure what to expect with what she says or what she does?

6. ❏ Are you not sure how to act when you're around your DIL because she doesn't really try to engage with you?

7. ❏ Does your DIL have your son tell you that she's upset about something you said or did, instead of telling you directly?

8. ❏ Does it seem that your DIL wants nothing to do with you, and she's very obvious about it?

9. ❏ Is your DIL polite and even pleasant when interacting with you, yet she makes no real effort to engage with you?

10. ❏ Do you feel as though you have to compete with your DIL's family when it comes to seeing your grandchildren – or even your own son?

11. ❏ Do you have to "gear up" to talk to or be around your DIL?

12. ❏ Are you unsure about how your relationship with your DIL is supposed to be?

13. ❏ Do you find yourself saying, "Why is she acting this way toward me?" Or "Why is she treating me like this?"

14. ❏ When you're around your DIL, do you start to doubt yourself in ways you never did before?

15. ❏ Do you feel as though your DIL makes no real effort to interact with you directly and that your interactions with her seem to be mostly through your son?

16. ❏ Does it feel as though you can't talk to your son the way you used to?

17. ❏ Do you notice your son pulling further away from the whole family – not just from you?

18. ❏ Do you try to look comfortable around your DIL, but in reality you can't relax around her?

19. ❏ Do you feel at a loss with what's going on between you and your DIL?

20. ❏ Does it seem that your DIL has no need for any type of family connection and that she's perfectly OK with that?

21. ❏ Do you feel as though your DIL is not really interested in improving the relationship between the two of you?

22. ❏ Does your DIL get upset when you attempt to help? (Or if she doesn't act upset with you, does she later say something to your son about being upset?)

23. ❏ Does your DIL seem to have a way of looking at things that's different from the way everyone else you know looks at them – to the point where it seems impossible to figure out how she perceives what she is doing?

24. ❏ Although your DIL is nice to you, are you confused as to why she has no interest in engaging with you?

25. ❏ Do you find yourself walking on eggshells around your DIL – not sure how to act or how she'll react to you?

26. ❏ Do you find that your son seems to make a lot of excuses for your DIL?

27. ❏ Do you find that you really don't take the initiative to interact with your DIL and that you'd rather just initiate interaction with your son?

28. ❏ Does it feel as though your DIL blows the smallest things out of proportion?

29. ❏ Does your DIL seem a little off, but you can't quite put your finger on what's up with her?

30. ❏ Do you feel like giving up on having expectations of any kind about your DIL?

31. ❏ Does it feel as though your DIL never lets you know when she's upset with you, but yet you often feel tension between the two of you?

32. ❏ Does your DIL make excuses for not spending time with you or with any of your son's side of the family?

33. ❏ Does it feel as if your son is more distant from you than he was before he got married?

Scoring Key for MILs Identifying Their DIL

For each character category below, circle the numbers that correspond to the question numbers you checked in the questionnaire. Note that the same numbers sometimes appear in more than one character category. When you're finished, count the number of circled numbers for each character – your DIL most likely belongs to the category where you circled the most numbers.

Doubting Donna:
1, 4, 5, 7, 10, 11, 13, 16, 18, 19, 22, 25, 28, 31, 33

Weird Wendy:
2, 5, 8, 11, 13, 14, 15, 17, 18, 19, 20, 23, 26, 27, 28, 29, 30, 32

Transitioned Tracy:
3, 6, 9, 10, 11, 12, 15, 18, 19, 21, 24, 30, 32, 33

Questionnaire for DILs Identifying Their MIL

Please check the statements that *best* fit how you feel or that *best* fit your situation with your MIL.

1. ❏ Do you hear a parental tone from your MIL that just makes you want to scream?

2. ❏ Does your MIL always make everything about *her*, even when it's not?

3. ❏ Do you feel frustrated with your MIL when you really need something from her and she's unavailable, yet when you don't need her she's all over you trying to "help"?

4. ❏ Does your MIL have an air about her that seems to reflect that she thinks she knows best – even though she may not say anything directly?

5. ❏ Do you feel as though you have to "gear up" just to be around your MIL or to talk to her?

6. ❏ Do you find you really don't like who your MIL is?

7. ❏ Does your MIL show up at your house uninvited, with no warning, and just walk right in?

8. ❏ Do you feel drained after talking with or spending any time with your MIL?

9. ❏ Does it seem as though your MIL tries too hard or is just somehow off in the way she interacts with you?

10. ❏ Do you find yourself getting edgy or irritable just knowing that you're going to be around your MIL?

11. ❏ Do you feel as though your MIL punishes you in some way when you don't do what she wants you to do?

12. ❏ Does it feel awkward at times when just you and your MIL are together?

13. ❏ Do you feel like screaming when your MIL acts as though she knows your husband better than you do?

14. ❏ Does your MIL say or act any way she wants to, with no concern about how it affects you?

15. ❏ Have you given up having expectations of your MIL?

16. ❏ Do you find yourself feeling hurt, frustrated or even angry with the way your MIL treats you?

17. ❏ Do you feel as though your MIL gets her way with everyone – and it drives you crazy?

18. ❏ Do you really have no desire to develop a relationship with your MIL?

19. ❏ Do you and your husband fight more often as the time gets closer to a visit from his mother?

20. ❏ Do you make a point of taking no real initiative to interact with your MIL, letting your husband deal with her whenever possible?

21. ❏ Do you get ticked off when your husband defends his mother instead of seeing your point of view?

22. ❏ Do you find yourself dumbstruck by some of your MIL's behavior?

23. ❏ Do you find yourself asking, "Why is she trying so hard? It feels intrusive."

24. ❏ Is your husband just not getting why you are so upset with his mother?

25. ❏ Do you dread the phone ringing when you know it's your MIL or do you check the caller ID before you answer, just in case it might be she?

26. ❏ Does your husband seem to go mute when you bring up your frustration with his mother?

27. ❏ Do you watch your husband turn into a little boy right before your eyes whenever he's around his mother?

28. ❏ Does it seem like your MIL tries to be hurtful toward you?

29. ❏ Does your husband ignore his mother's behavior most of the time, seeming not to be affected by her craziness the way that you are?

30. ❏ Do you feel that it's important for your children to have a relationship with your MIL, even if you don't want to have a relationship with her yourself?

31. ❏ Do you notice that your husband doesn't call his mother back when she leaves messages?

32. ❏ Do you think your MIL is pretty much OK, yet you still don't want a close relationship with her?

33. ❏ Have you noticed that your husband doesn't make much effort to interact with his mother and that his mother does all the initiating?

Scoring Key for DILs Identifying Their MIL

For each character category below, circle the numbers that correspond to the question numbers you checked in the questionnaire. Note that the same numbers sometimes appear in more than one character category. When you're finished, count the number of circled numbers for each character – your MIL most likely belongs to the category where you circled the most numbers.

Mothering Margaret:
1, 4, 5, 7, 10, 13, 16, 19, 21, 24, 26, 27

Off-the-Wall Wanda:
2, 5, 6, 8, 10, 11, 14, 15, 16, 17, 18, 20, 22, 25, 28, 29, 30, 31, 33

Uncertain Sara:
3, 5, 6, 9, 12, 15, 18, 19, 20, 23, 30, 32

Resources

If you are interested in more information or assistance with the MIL/ DIL relationship, please go to Dr. Brann's website www.DrDeannaBrann.com where you can ask questions, get answers, and learn much, much more.

You will also find a variety of products and services at www.DrDeannaBrann.com on the *Offers* page for both MILs and DILs that are geared to give you the personalized help you may need:

* Downloads of various skills to help change your in-law relationship
* One-on-one phone consultation packages
* Various one-on-one coaching opportunities
* Download of the C.A.R.E. System Program

Information for live events, seminars and small workshops can be found on the *Speaking* page of Dr. Brann's website— www.DrDeannaBrann.com

To have Dr. Brann speak at any of your groups or organizations, please contact Dr. Brann through the *Speaking* page on her website— www.DrDeannaBrann.com

****

If you would like to share your story about your mother-in-law/ daughter-in-law relationship and how you changed or are changing your relationship, please email your story to MyStory@DrDeannaBrann.com.

Deanna Brann, Ph.D.

With more than 25 years of experience in the mental health field, licensed clinical psychotherapist Deanna Brann specializes in communication skills, interpersonal relationships, and conflict resolution. So when her relationship with her own daughter-in-law began a dizzyingly downward spiral after the birth of her first grandchild, no one could have been more shocked than she was. The typical mother-in-law/daughter-in-law relationship, she soon realized, involves several unique twists and turns that she didn't see coming and was ill equipped to deal with—even as a psychotherapist!

Committed to exploring the nuances of mother-in-law/daughter-in-law dynamics, Dr. Brann began to conduct extensive qualitative research and discovered she was hardly alone in having such challenges. As a result of the behavioral patterns she identified, the different kinds of mothers-in-law and daughters-in-law she found, and the tools she developed to navigate these specific individuals with skill and grace, Dr. Brann discovered a way for both mothers-in-law and daughters-in-law to peacefully coexist. Not only has she transformed her own relationship with her daughter-in-law, but Dr. Brann has also helped countless other in-laws stop the cycle of frustration, anxiety, and anger they so often find themselves trapped inside. As she shares in *Reluctantly Related: Secrets to Getting Along With Your Mother-in-Law or Daughter-in-Law,* these women are able to grow more comfortable with—and sometimes even close to—each other in ways they never before imagined.

Dr. Brann holds a Master of Science degree in clinical psychology and a Ph.D. in psychobiological anthropology—and she's been a mother-in-law for more than 17 years and a daughter-in-law for more than 15. Through her various Skills DVDs and downloads, one-on-one consultations and coaching, as well as her in-depth teleseminars, live events, and workshops, she teaches mothers-in-law and daughters-in-law the techniques for shifting their thinking to a new level, inspiring powerful insights that help them change their in-law relationship for the better—forever. Dr. Brann is also the author of a cartoon book, *Mothers-in-Law and Daughters-in-Law Say the Darndest Things!* Further, she is a nationally known speaker on the subject of mother-in-law/daughter-in-law relationships. Go to her interactive website, www. DrDeannaBrann.com, where she specifically addresses mother-in-law/daughter-in-law issues.

CPSIA information can be obtained at www.ICGtesting.com
Printed in the USA
BVOW01s0717140813

328218BV00008B/105/P